WHAT OTHERS ARE SAYING A

Tom Bertling's "American ⁞
the Myth" sounds an alarm to all parents and teachers of deaf
children on the predicament in which American education of
the deaf finds itself. Hopefully, this book will enable school
administrators to recognize that teaching English reading and
writing is the prime purpose for the existence of their tax-
supported institutions.

-Ed. Scouten, Retired
Distinguished Educator of the Deaf
GALLAUDET UNIVERSITY, NTID

ASL may have a grammar and linguistic structure of
its own, but every literate deaf person, young or old, whom I
have met, taught, and worked with communicated to me in
Signed English *on the whole. Thus, I would assume that, as*
Noah Webster did with his "American Dictionary of the
English Language," advocates of ASL are mainly being
patriotic! Hopefully, this collection of illuminating essays by
well-known and established scholars will send a "wake-up
call" to the guardians of education -- teachers and admin-
istrators -- in our schools and programs for deaf learners.

-Dr. Robert F. Panara,
Professor Emeritus
NTID/ROCHESTER INSTITUTE OF
TECHNOLOGY

ASL: SHATTERING THE MYTH

Tom Bertling, editor of "American Sign Language: Shattering the Myth," has for many years advocated truthful disclosure of certain unpleasant realities of life in Deaf Society. In this collection of essays written by respected deaf scholars who place themselves squarely in front of the steamroller of ASL radicalism, Bertling focuses light and reason upon the internal inconsistencies, absence of scholarship, and conflict of interest of leaders of the Deaf-World. These insights, which represent the position of the large majority of grass roots deaf people, provide an important background for anyone interested in a balanced view of the current atmosphere of academic repression, especially at Gallaudet University.

-Thomas J. Balkany, MD, FACS, FAAP
Hotchkiss Distinguished Professor and
Vice Chairman, Otolaryngology
UNIVERSITY OF MIAMI

ASL: SHATTERING THE MYTH

The brain of a deaf person is no different from that of a hearing person. With the proper input and attention, all deaf people can read and write in English at the same level as their hearing peers. Deaf students in Europe achieve equal language skills with their hearing peers, even in several languages. The USA can do the same, by removing outdated educational methods, and following scientific research instead of ideologies and opinions.

Tom Bertling has done an excellent job of compiling the ignored and almost forgotten message that deaf individuals must learn to read and write English fluently, for successful careers in our modern, information-based society.

> *-Paulette R. Caswell, M.S.-TESL, J.D.*
> *PhD Prgm, Int'l-Intercultural Studies*
> ***UNIVERSITY OF SOUTHERN CALIFORNIA***

Tom Bertling provides a valuable service to all educators, parents of deaf children and those interested in the continuing controversy over the use of ASL. In a unique and remarkable collection of wise and moderate voices he unmasks the politics and the mythology of ASL and yet shows respect for ASL itself. How can we thank Tom Bertling save in constant hoping that his work will be widely read and provide a moderating influence in developing educational programs geared to the needs of the individual deaf child.

> *-Arnold B. Adelman, Director*
> ***SPEECH AND HEARING FOUNDATION OF MASS., INC.***

ASL: SHATTERING THE MYTH

EDITOR'S NOTE:

    I'd like to offer a special note of appreciation to Prof. Frances Parsons, not only for her contributions and for access to her archives, but for having the foresight to preserve many of these essential documents that are now simply indispensable. A better future lies ahead for deaf children as a result of her sticking to her convictions in the face of overwhelming adversity.

    I'd also like to thank Dr. Otto Menzel for his contribution and his generous expert assistance with this book. Other notes of appreciation go to Dr. Truman Stelle, Dr. Donald Moores and Patrick Seamans for their contributions. Additional thanks go to Paulette Caswell, and of course, to Valerie Jo and Rikki Sage as always.

PUBLISHER'S NOTE:

    The opinions voiced by the contributors to this book are theirs alone and do not necessarily reflect those held by the publisher or the publishing company. We do support one's right to express an opinion and we stand behind all our writers in this regard. We strongly support our society's intolerance for censorship and wholly oppose any attempt to impose restrictions on our rights to free speech and freedom of the press.

    *There is very little agreement among all the factions involved with the education of the deaf child. Parents must explore all possibilities and options, then make the best decision for **their** child.*

    It is not our intent to identify or ridicule anyone personally in this book. Only individuals who have already publicly spoken out or have become part of the published public record may have been identified.

COVER ILLUSTRATION: The drawing of Laurent Clerc on the cover of this book was done by the internationally renowned deaf artist Richard Z. Wren. This portrait was drawn from a statue of Clerc that stands on the Gallaudet University campus near Fowler Hall.

KODIAK MEDIA GROUP: Publishers of vital educational and scholastic material. Available domestically and worldwide through most major book wholesalers and distributors, or you may contact the publisher directly. Large quantity educational discounts available.

AMERICAN SIGN LANGUAGE: SHATTERING THE MYTH

Essays by:

FRANCES M. PARSONS
LARRY G. STEWART

With additional contributions from:

OTTO J. MENZEL
DONALD F. MOORES
PATRICK W. SEAMANS
TRUMAN W. STELLE

Edited by TOM BERTLING

KODIAK MEDIA GROUP

ASL: SHATTERING THE MYTH

First edition published 1998

10 9 8 7 6 5 4 3 2 1

For further information contact: KODIAK MEDIA GROUP
                                     P.O. Box 1029-B3
                                     Wilsonville, Oregon 97070

SAN: 297.9993

ISBN: 0-9637813-5-9

U.S. Library of Congress Catalog Card Number: 98-66201

PUBLISHER'S CATALOGING IN PUBLICATION DATA:
Edited by Tom Bertling.
American Sign Language: Shattering the Myth.
        Bibliography information.
        1. Deafness--United States. 2. Deaf--Education of deaf children.
        3. Deaf--Means of communication. 4. Sign Language and
        Linguistics. 5. Cultural issues. I Title.

Kodiak Media Group is a privately-owned company and receives no private or public (including non-profit) special-interest funding or grants.

kmyth98/c/486/pent233

CONTENTS

ASL: SHATTERING THE MYTH

Frances M. Parsons

Prof. Parsons, also known as Gallaudet University's "World Ambassador," was a professor of art history there until her recent retirement. For over two decades, she has traveled the world extensively, sowing the seeds for future students of Gallaudet. She has set foot in more schools for the deaf worldwide than anyone else, urging deaf students to seek a better future for themselves and their homelands.

An outspoken advocate for deaf children, Prof. Parsons has written extensively on matters of deaf education and communicational issues. She is the author of two books, *Sounds of the Stars* and *I Didn't Hear the Dragon Roar [Both are out of print]*. The latter is a highly acclaimed journal of her unusual solo odyssey through China, detailing an experience rarely achieved by Westerners, let alone a deaf individual. She is also a writer of countless magazine and deaf periodical articles.

A graduate of the California School for the Deaf in Berkeley, and Gallaudet University, she received her Master's Degree from the University of Maryland, and an "ABD" ("All But Dissertation") from George Washington University and Howard University.

Larry G. Stewart

The late Dr. Stewart, a psychologist by profession, was a professor of psychology at Gallaudet University until his untimely death in 1993. A 1953 graduate of the Texas School for the Deaf, he earned his Bachelor's degree from Gallaudet, his Master's from the University of Missouri and his Doctorate from the University of Arizona. Prior to his position at Gallaudet, he was a superintendent of a state residential school for the deaf.

Known for his outspoken advocacy for deaf children, Dr. Stewart was nationally recognized for his work in many programs, including presentations at major symposiums and conferences in the United States and abroad. He has written extensively in the rehabilitation and mental health field and possessed a unique broad background in the field of deafness education.

Toward the end of his life he expressed concern about many of the deaf cultural and language philosophies and their potential effect on the future of deaf children. Dr. Stewart's colleagues do agree that if he were alive today, he would have gladly agreed to this compilation.

INTRODUCTION

Parents of deaf children, professionals and educators of the deaf, and members of the hearing society in general are awash in a rather one-sided view of deaf culture, and in particular, American Sign Language (or ASL). In short, things are not what they seem.

In an attempt to bring the general knowledge of these emotional cultural and language issues towards a more balanced center, we have compiled the essays of two of the most vocal advocates for English-based signing who have stood by their convictions despite finding themselves in the middle of a firestorm at the world-wide center of deaf culture - - Gallaudet University.

Frances M. Parsons and Larry G. Stewart both possessed the wisdom and courage to question and raise skepticism at a time when many of their deaf peers and colleagues were rushing to board what some have described as a runaway train. Biographic information about them can be found on page 8.

We have the privilege to present a few additional contributions by other esteemed and highly regarded professionals on these matters. All of these writers venture into the heart of deaf language and cultural issues and reward us with the kind of critical thinking and skepticism largely absent from many of the proponents of ASL-based learning for the deaf.

ASL: SHATTERING THE MYTH

Keep in mind that none of these individuals have called for the demise of deaf culture or the elimination of ASL usage outside the classroom. It would be (and has always been) a mistake to assume all proponents of English-based signing are "anti-ASL."

In an effort not to daunt the readers, we have avoided the use of the many acronyms used to indentify the numerous methods of signing that are based on English or in English-word-order (Such as SEE, TC, ASE, sim-com, Cued Speech etc.) Instead, where necessary, we have simply referred to them as English-based signing or English-word-order.

We wish here to give the reader a little background on the so-called Bi-Bi (Bilingual-Bicultural) method of educating the deaf. This popular method, which originated with ASL advocates, supposedly teaches the deaf child ASL first; then after fluency is attained, the child is taught English. Speech (if at all) is taught much later. This concept has gained popularity among many despite the fact there is no evidence that Bi-Bi works. Indeed, "Bilingual-Bicultural" is probably a misnomer as the emphasis is clearly on ASL, and English is considered only secondary. In reality, many say, what is being done is in no sense bilingual or bicultural. They are teaching ASL, period.

Some have pointed out the originators of the Bi-Bi method prefer that pupils not learn English, rather finding it expedient to pretend that they do -- and not through English itself but by more and more instruction in wordless ASL. It is impractical and inefficient to try to teach one language using another, when the language of instruction (ASL) is so grossly different in grammar and in every other way from the language being taught (English). The goal is simply unattainable.

We must also remember that *"deaf culture,"* the concept used fondly by deaf militants and chauvinists, is not an

10

anthropological phenomenon, but rather, a purely political *creation*.

There is a school of thought that believes there is a difference between "ASL" and "American Sign Language." This apparently has something to do with specific definitions used in various "communicational policies." But for the editorial purposes of this book, ASL and American Sign Language are one and the same.

It is entirely possible the popularity of ASL and it's acceptance among many members of the mainstream society, including educators and politicians, is the result of an enormous misunderstanding. Many believe that American Sign Language is a "signing version of English," or American Signed-*English* Language. This, of course, is not true. The fact is: ASL is entirely different from English, to the point where English usage is discouraged, disregarded and deliberately avoided. This misunderstanding has resulted in acceptance of ASL in many educational programs along with public funding to support these programs. If more understood that ASL was being taught at the expense of (or even instead of) English, public support for ASL would evaporate.

Although some of these essays were written earlier in this decade, they are just as valid today as when they were first written, in some cases, even more so.

As we enter the new millennium, these essays will be substantiated by our deaf children of the future. Only when English is returned to prominence in our deaf schools and programs can we truly begin to see an end to the "dark ages" of deaf education.

CHAPTER ONE

THE ESSAYS OF LARRY G. STEWART

TO:	All Faculty Members	November 5, 1990
FROM:	Larry G. Stewart	
SUBJECT:	Another (!) Open Letter	

My fellow Faculty members, trusting that you will favor me with your patience, I make bold to share some thoughts for your consideration this fine November day.

For the 125th time (or is it 126th?), November envelops what has become known the world over as Kendall Green. Those gorgeous, flaming colors of autumn now swathe the trees and bushes of the campus as the days shorten and dusk descends quickly of an evening. Soon, quiet winter will be upon the land once graced by those noble giants, E.M. Gallaudet and Laurent Clerc.

Yet wait a while; let winter's slumber desist for the nonce. Just as the trees that dot the campus flame brightly as if in protest of their impending winter-long slumber, so too are the intellectual sons and daughters of Gallaudet and Clerc beginning to protest and burn with the fires unleashed by unbridled rhetoric over -- of course -- communication issues!

That fierce, feminine, feisty, globe-trotting fighter for deaf folks all over the world, Frances "Peggy" Parsons, recently erupted in all her flaming grandeur. Sending forth her views in no-holds-barred, penetrating, lava-like, brook-no-nonsense rhetoric, Peggy literally told the Faculty o' the Green to "cut the nonsense and get back to good, old-fashioned clear communication." Said she, "Can (as in can the tuna) the ASL extremism and wake up to good old reality before it hits you on the head."

Yet, stay you! Were that not wisdom enough for the ages, still another eruption occurred recently on the Green in that dastardly, dangerous, deity-defying volcano-pocked landscape known to some as "One-Size-Fits-All Communication Strip" (shortened to "One-Size-Fits-All" due to translation difficulties).

Another worldly, wise, widely-traveled worker on the Green, yon honorable Harvey Goodstein, o' him-o'-the-spark-that-lit-the-forge-that-cast-the-new-Faculty-Communication policy, once again trumpeted forth his sage interpretations and observations on the "One-Size-Fits-All" landscape. Suggested good Harvey, among other things and with many wise words, Kendall Green Faculty members need to revise and clarify for this year the recently revised and clarified Faculty Communication Policy that was clarified last year.

And so, on this glorious autumn day, we of the venerable Gallaudet University Faculty find ourselves standing on the historic threshold (or abysmal drop, depending on what? -- one's current level of Sign communication proficiency?) of voting for or against a proposed new Faculty Communication Proficiency Evaluation procedure.

I like the present Gallaudet University Faculty Communication Policy. I voted in favor of this new policy last Spring. I encouraged others to vote in favor of it. My feelings haven't changed since then, either. I still believe the policy is flexible, that it is clear, and that it will ultimately serve Gallaudet very well. While the policy is certainly no "Open Sesame" incantation that will suddenly enable us all to understand one another, it is free of political agendas and it does not make a mockery of academic freedom. I will vote against any change to the current policy until I see a proposal that improves on the current one (and I haven't seen such an improvement yet). I do understand when some wish to simplify the complex reality of communication among deaf people, for doing so is comforting and we can all certainly use any comfort we can get considering the current national and international scenes. However, we at Gallaudet cannot have it both ways; we are either a university of excellence where critical thinking and the search for the truth are paramount concerns of all faculty members, or we are like any other organization where each of us "picks and chooses" what we wish to consider as truth based on political agendas.

Over the past six months I have traveled widely across the United States. Everywhere I have gone I have had some deaf people AND some hearing people approach me and ask, "What's wrong with Gallaudet? Why is Gallaudet so hung-up on ASL? Isn't Gallaudet supposed to teach deaf students English?" Some people have heard of Gallaudet's new communication policy and praised it. Others, who have heard, erroneously, that Gallaudet supports only ASL, have expressed alarm and warned me that many schools, especially mainstream schools, will stop sending their graduates to Gallaudet if all students are forced to learn ASL-only. Some deaf adults have expressed concern that the government will stop supporting Gallaudet if it becomes exclusive and emphasizes only ASL.

This past summer, the Board of Directors of the National Association of the Deaf voted to commend the

University Faculty for its new Faculty Communication Policy. A letter to this effect was sent to the Chair of the University Faculty, Dr. William J. Marshall.

One experienced parent of a deaf adult, whom I have known over 20 years, recently wrote to me: "The ability of a deaf person to write appropriate English with proper grammar and syntax is essential for acceptance and success in the hearing world. The inability to express oneself with appropriate English greatly decreases the chance for employment, improvement in employment, and acceptance."

According to available prevalence information, there are over two million deaf citizens in the U.S. Available information appears to indicate that possibly 80 percent of them do not use sign communication at all, let alone ASL as defined by linguists. What does this signify for Gallaudet faculty? I propose to you that it is certainly not intended to minimize the importance of ASL, for I feel that we all need to accept ASL as an essential aspect in the education of deaf students at all levels. However, equally importantly, it DOES signify equally the reality of the crucial need of each faculty member for skill in the use of a variety of communication approaches with deaf students at Gallaudet. Any communication policy or evaluation system that does not recognize the reality of the diverse communication needs of deaf students at Gallaudet must ultimately be viewed as being one based not upon truth concerning the real needs of deaf students but upon political agendas.

The Communication Proficiency Evaluation proposal recently developed by Committee A and supported by the University Faculty looks good to me. It has my support. It is surely not perfect; there remain problems to be worked out but we can do it.

ASL: SHATTERING THE MYTH

Various and sundry Faculty members are thinking deeply this day, ere the Faculty meeting begins, mulling over their own thoughts about the barren "One-Size-fits-All" landscape.

One faculty member, touched somewhat with mild pedantry, while standing at the abysmal drop and peering down in mournful thought, put the private thinking of many a faculty member in a nutshell: "Why, how can I vote on evaluating American Sign Language when it has not been operationally defined the way I want it defined (and, incidentally, the way I happen to use it)? Come on, now! Didn't they define English before anyone could use it meaningfully!" (Note: Do not flinch unduly; "they" as used here is pure rhetoric and we need not locate the folks in question for an accounting).

Another faculty member, standing at another vantage point of the abysmal drop (and who coincidentally doesn't use Sign too well), exclaimed, "Look here now! Who says Gallaudet University exists to serve only deaf students who use Sign communication? What about oral deaf folks who need faculty who can communicate with them? Where is that written, I ask you, that Signs must be evaluated but not oral communication skills?"

A third faculty member, standing at what she saw as the glorious threshold, announced proudly (in fluent Signs, of course): "Finally, after 125 (or is it 126?) years, more new Faculty folks around here are going to learn to use Sign better, else before long they will surely and purely put on their traveling shoes! And, hey, who says we need to learn oral skills? Students have to learn Sign communication if they are going to stay at Gallaudet!"

A fourth faculty member, standing at still another vantage point at the threshold of glory, proclaimed vigorously (in fluent Sign, right?) that ". . . a new evaluation policy that demands at least Intermediate Plus skills in Sign will mean quite a few folks around these parts are going to be embarrassed into taking the SCPI *[Sign Communication Proficiency Interview, a communication evaluation tool used at Gallaudet to determine merit increases and/or a promotion]* since they haven't taken it or anything else for years and years!"

Martin Buber (1970, *I and Thou* [translation by Walter Kaufmann.] New York: Charles Scribner's Sons, pp. 9 - 10), once wrote:

> "Man's world is manifold, and his attitudes are manifold. What is manifold is often frightening because it is not neat and simple. Men prefer to forget how many possibilities are open to them.
> They like to be told there are two worlds and two ways. This is comforting because it is so tidy. Almost always one way turns out to be common and the other one is celebrated as superior.
> Those who tell of two ways and praise one are recognized as prophets or great teachers. They save men from confusion and hard choices . . .
> To walk far on this path may be difficult, but the choice is easy, and to hear the celebration of this path is pleasant.
> *Mundus vult decipi:* the world wants to be deceived. The truth is too complex and frightening . . .
> What is wanted is an oversimplification, a reduction of a multitude of possibilities to only two . . ."

Did Buber possibly have in mind such bipolar thinking as is prevalent on the Green, whereby ASL is simplistically yet popularly defined by some, whereas others perceive a complex reality in the sign communication (American sign language) used among the nation's over two million deaf citizens?

This Open Letter closes with a short story, offered as a caveat to those of us who are tempted to make unwise compromises along the way in the wording of Gallaudet's

communication policy and in the Faculty Communication
Proficiency Evaluation procedures.

Ishmael was a desert nomad; he and his camel traveled the
vast Sahara Desert regularly as Ishmael pursued his work as a
trader. With him Ishmael of course carried a small tent, for the
nights on the vast desert could be incredibly and bitterly cold. One
night as he and his camel paused at a lonely oasis deep in the
isolated and barren desert, Ishmael noted the night was
uncommonly cold even for the desert at that time of the year.
Shivering almost uncontrollably, he tethered the camel securely
beside the tent, decided to forego dinner, and instead climbed
inside the tent, wrapping himself as warmly as he could and
snuggling down for the cold night ahead. Shortly, Ishmael was
sleeping fitfully. Some time after midnight he was startled into
abrupt wakefulness by the cold nose of his camel against his face,
who whimpered and asked forlornly if he could not put his head
inside the tent, it was so unbelievably cold outside. In empathy,
Ishmael painfully shifted himself over to make room in the small,
cramped tent for his camel's icy, shaking head. Soon, both were
sleeping fitfully. And yet, not long after, Ishmael again awakened
to the cold nose of his camel. The camel, piteously distraught,
gnashed his teeth and pleaded, in view of the bitter cold outside.
His master, Ishmael, allowed him to do the unthinkable, to put his
long neck and bony front legs and hooves inside the small but
warm tent. Grumbling with irritation, yet all too aware of the
intense cold, Ishmael scrunched himself into a ball as the front
part of the ice-cold, smelly camel moved inside the small tent,
almost filling it. Again, Ishmael fell into a cold, fitful sleep.
Outside, the temperature plummeted even further. The wind
started to pick up, wafting fine grains of sand into the tent as the
wind chill factor took its toll of man and beast. Slowly, ever so
slowly, the miserable camel inched its body forward, ever forward,
seeking the warmth inside the small, lonely tent on the vast desert
in the icy black night. The seemingly interminable night wore on.
More and more of the tent was filled by the smelly, shivering
camel. Slowly, ever so slowly, the now deeply-sleeping Ishmael,
dead to the world, was inched out into the cold, uncaring night by

the camel's movements. The night wore on. The stars dimmed. At last Ishmael, almost frozen, fluttered open his eyes to find himself outside, covered with gritty, icy sand, all alone. Inside the tent slept the camel, warm and peaceful.

[Reprinted with permission from Gallaudet University]

Gallaudet University   September 13, 1991
Department of Psychology

Dear Editor:

I was appalled to read the *ON THE GREEN [A Gallaudet publication]* article concerning the decision to use "sign without voice" and "ASL-only in the classrooms" at MSSD and KDES *[Model Secondary School (residential) for the Deaf, Kendall Demonstration Elementary School, both located on the Gallaudet campus]* This prompts me to wonder how little we have truly learned since the infamous ICED *[International Conference of Educators of the Deaf]* in Milan in 1880, when oralism was proclaimed by the world's professionals in deaf education as THE answer to the educational needs of deaf children. Ironically, today the pendulum has swung in the opposite direction: signing without voice, particularly ASL (or the version of ASL that doesn't follow English), has seemingly replaced oralism as THE one great answer in the education of all deaf children. What is tragic is that neither of these two polarities -- ASL or Oralism -- serves the needs of the great majority of deaf children, simply because these needs vary so much among individuals.

KDES and MSSD are located on the campus of Gallaudet University, the flagship campus of American higher education for deaf citizens; Gallaudet is the pride and joy of the deaf community. Both KDES and MSSD were legislated to serve as *national model demonstration schools,* and as such the two schools are responsible for representing the very best and reliable models in the education of deaf children this nation has to offer. Thus the decision at KDES-MSSD was, for me as a member of the Gallaudet professional community, a source of great embarrassment, for it is nothing short of mind-boggling to note that the decision to stop using voice while signing, and to use ASL-only in the classroom, is built upon a foundation that is starkly without benefit of respectable substantive educational learning theory or solid prior research findings on instructional practices and outcomes (as repeatedly documented by Professor Donald Moores, myself and others in previous communications on this campus).

At this time, I challenge MSSD-KDES leadership to produce for this campus community to review any research plan worthy of the name designed to study the dependent and independent variables associated with the main processes and outcomes in this new "grand experiment" with deaf children and their parents, including controls for the characteristics of the deaf children and teachers that constitute the samples under "study."

Lest my position be misconstrued as "anti-ASL," I, like others around the country and many on this campus, am a staunch supporter of the use of clear sign communication with deaf children and adults, regardless of what a particular brand of sign is called (ASL, Signed English, SEE 1, SEE 2, SEE Heinz 57, or whatever). However, we are also supporters of the use of other forms of communication that do the job for individual deaf children and their teachers, and most of all we are supporters of the human rights of all children and teachers. This automatically makes us foes of any school or teacher or administrator or activist who would restrict the range of communication options available to deaf children and their teachers in the name of ASL, sign-without-voice, oralism, or any other single method.

Today someone told me, "But, signing without voice leads to clearer signing." To this I say, "Perhaps, but this gives us no right to burden deaf children with unskilled communicators, nor require that teachers who do not sign clearly obtain more training on their own time. Don't allow them to practice at the expense of the children."

Today another person remarked to me that the administrator who allowed this new policy at KDES-MSSD is courageous. To this I say: "No, that administrator appears to lack understanding of the right of deaf children to have access to all methods of communication."

Today still another person, an administrator who supports this new KDES-MSSD "policy-that-is-not-policy" told me, after I had argued that the policy reflects no consideration for educational research standards, that "Even the Devil can quote the Scriptures." To this I say, "And who exactly is the Devil in this whole affair?"

During the two years I have been at Gallaudet I have heard argument after argument after argument about "ASL," about "deaf culture," about "the failure of deaf education," and about "the need to use ASL from the cradle to the grave" for all deaf people, but all in a vacuum devoid of substantive theory or empirical research evidence to support any position. Even the recent MSA *[Middle States Association, a college accreditation agency]* evaluation of Gallaudet questioned the use of the term "culture," as in "deaf culture," to describe the unique phenomena of sign communication and the deaf community.

U.S. taxpayers have been spending millions and millions and millions of dollars to support Gallaudet and KDES and

MSSD. While most of us support the Gallaudet-KDES-MSSD programs, neither reason, common sense, nor sound professional judgment can support spending millions of tax dollars each year in support of policies of instruction for deaf children that are not buttressed by any substantial educational research. For us on the Green to support such an unwise course is simply intolerable in the midst of a campus which is supposed to represent the very best in educational methodology for deaf children and adults -- including quality of research -- the world has to offer.

I call on others in the Gallaudet community to join together in protest of this new practice at KDES-MSSD and demand a return to a flexible, child-centered communication policy. I suspect that if we don't get our act in order on this issue, the public will do it for us.

Larry G. Stewart, Ed.D.
Professor (and tax payer)

[Reprinted with permission from Gallaudet University]

September 23, 1991

QUESTIONS FROM PROFESSOR LARRY STEWART, PSYCHOLOGY DEPARTMENT

As a faculty member, I am increasingly concerned about the accurateness and possible implications of reports circulating on the campus concerning the programmatic use of sign without voice and ASL-Only in the classrooms of Gallaudet University's Precollege Programs.

Gallaudet University's mission at all levels includes teaching, research, and service to both deaf and hard of hearing citizens, and such a constituency demands a broad-based communication philosophy and a variety of modalities. The question is raised, then, as to the appropriateness of instruction which concentrates on the communication needs of only a segment of the deaf population.

Public Law 94-142 requires a written individualized education plan (IEP) for each school-age disabled child, including deaf children, to be developed according to the needs of the individual child as determined at an interdisciplinary case conference in which the child's parents or guardians are afforded opportunity for full participation. The question is thus raised whether an appropriate IEP is in place for each child throughout a school that adopts a blanket policy of "signs with no voice and ASL-only in the classroom," on a programmatic basis.

Our nation encourages diversification in curricular and instructional approaches in our schools, and values the individuality of each student and teacher. The question is therefore raised as to whether restricting teachers and children to the use of only one form of interpersonal communication is consistent with these basic American values.

There is no professionally recognized, authoritative, or otherwise definitive evidence one way or another concerning the effectiveness of any specific method of communication or specific language in the education of deaf children. Any new programmatic approach for demonstrating the efficacy of a particular method of communication or use of a different language should, logically, therefore entail a comprehensive program plan describing relevant components of the new approach, including an appropriate evaluative research (outcomes) plan designed to assess the efficacy of the new approach. Is there such a plan in place?

ASL: SHATTERING THE MYTH

The participating teachers, students and/or their parents need to be informed concerning the risks and benefits of the new approach consistent with laws and regulations concerning full disclosure and informed consent. Has this been the case?

[Stewart attached the following to his September 23, 1991 memo.]

BACKGROUND ISSUES FOR SIGN WITHOUT VOICE, ASL-ONLY IN THE CLASSROOM, AND IMPLICATIONS FOR GALLAUDET UNIVERSITY

I. From the 1991-1992 Gallaudet University Undergraduate Catalog:

A. The Mission of Gallaudet University

"The mission of Gallaudet University is to serve as a comprehensive, multipurpose institution of higher education for *deaf and hard of hearing citizens* of the United States and of the world. In addition to its undergraduate and graduate academic programs, the University also offers *national demonstration elementary and secondary educational programs* . . ." (Emphasis added) (p.3)

B. The Use of Sign Language, Speech, and English at Gallaudet University

"Gallaudet University is the only liberal arts university in the world designed exclusively for *deaf and hard of hearing students.* Communication among faculty, staff, and students, whether in or out of the classroom, is *through the use of both sign language and written and spoken English.* As a result, students are able to participate fully in all aspects of campus life and thereby acquire the comprehensive education and experience that is the goal of a liberal arts education." (Emphasis added) (p. 3)

C. Instruction, Research and Service Goals of Gallaudet University

"Gallaudet University is committed to providing instruction in the arts and sciences that are vital to the development of the intellect; *to conducting research aimed at enhancing the lives of deaf and hard of hearing individuals;* and to serving deaf and hard of hearing people, their families, their friends, and the professionals who work with them." (Emphases added) (p.3)

24

ASL: SHATTERING THE MYTH

II. From the report of the Commission on Education of the Deaf, *Toward Equality: Education of the Deaf,* February 1988, p. 87:

"Gallaudet University (GU), in addition to its on-Campus educational activities, has a national mission. *GU's charge, through its Pre-college Programs, is to conduct research, develop educational materials and techniques and disseminate the resulting products with a view to improving other educational programs for the deaf across the country."* (p. 87)

"The Congress asked the General Accounting Office (GAO) to survey the Pre-College Programs -- not to judge their quality -- but rather to report what activities are carried out, how research projects are monitored and evaluated, how costs are accounted for, how well research results are disseminated and products marketed, and to suggest improvements. GAO found no satisfactory system at GU for determining the costs of its national outreach mission as distinct from its on-campus education, as well as a *lack of internal controls for approving and monitoring research projects.* We believe a more precise degree of accountability is required when public money is being spent; and, moreover, that setting up a better system requires the kind of thinking that is bound to enhance rather than inhibit research creativity." (p. 87)

"We also recommend that *public comment and a peer review process become part of research plan development and project selection at GU* and NTID *[National Technical Institute for the Deaf, located in Rochester, N.Y.]."* (Emphasis added) (p. 87)

In a GAO review of Pre-College Programs, it was reported that "The Pre-College programs *lack adequate internal controls for approving and monitoring research projects . . . Pre-College programs were not able to produce documentation on many of the research projects being conducted. Procedures for reviewing and evaluating research projects were likewise informal and largely undocumented.* (p. 89)

More generally, GAO reported that *". . . GU lacks an oversight procedure for selecting, conducting, and monitoring research, development, and evaluation activities."* (p. 92) (Emphasis added)

III. From a recent follow-up report (F. Bowe, 1991, *Approaching Equality: Education of the Deaf.)*

ASL: SHATTERING THE MYTH

In responding to the COED'S *[Council on Education of the Deaf, agency that set teacher standards]* Recommendation 16, (that Congress should amend the Education of the Deaf Act to set certain priorities at the Kendall Demonstration Elementary School and the Model Secondary School for the Deaf, require annual reports to the Congress and the President, and require an evaluation and report every five years by the Department of Education's liaison office), Bowe's 1991 comments included:

"COED believes (in 1988) that MSSD was doing well at what it was trying to do *but that to a large extent it was trying to do the wrong things. We wanted it to be more of a "model" for the nation -- doing what the field most needed it to do . . .*

It is important that these schools respond to the priority needs of the nation's educators; *unless they do so, the field's support for these schools will continue to erode.* The priorities KDES and MSSD should meet were specified in *Toward Equality.*" (p. 33) (Emphasis added)

[Reprinted with permission from Gallaudet University]

Gallaudet Research Institute   October 10, 1991

MEMORANDUM

To: Nancy Shook, *[KDES Principal]*
       Michael Deninger *[Dean of Gallaudet]*
From: Don Moores, *[Professor at Gallaudet]*
       Larry Stewart
Re: **Communication Policies and Practices**

As you may be aware, we have expressed some confusion and concern over development and implementation of the PCP *[Precollege Programs]* communication policy. As long term colleagues and friends, with careers devoted to the welfare of deaf children, we would like to raise some issues with you for discussion as you develop plans for pilot studies. Although we are sure that you are well aware of this, we first want to state that we support the use of ASL both inside and outside of class. What concerns us is that flexibility and the concept of child-centered individual educational programs be maintained.

Related to the policy is the crying need for research on the issue of communication with deaf children. Frankly, we are worried that incorrect information is being distributed. For example, we are enclosing a page from the 9/27 KDES Weekly Parent Bulletin. The section begins, "Teaching a deaf child the language of signs will help him learn English later, reports a research team from the University of Pittsburgh." Later the researchers are identified as Stokoe, Casterline, and Croneberg. Now, we all know that Stokoe, et. al. were never at Pitt and that they never did the type of research described! In fact, we know of no research at Pitt that fits the description. And of course, we know "sign language" is not at all synonymous with ASL.

Related to this, in a 9/3/91 letter to KDES parents and guardians a statement is made ". . . a growing number of research studies have described the power and strength of this language (ASL) for instruction." This language was repeated in a 10/2/91 "Dean Talk" memo to PCP faculty and staff. Our problem, quite simply, is that we do not know of any research, with one exception, on the use of ASL for instruction. In the 1990 Hofstra University Conference on the Educational Use of ASL, representatives from the two programs most identified with ASL instruction, Fremont and the Learning Center, stated they had no research on the subject. Further, except for the work of David Stewart at Michigan State University, no other research on instruction was identified. The work by David Stewart which has been going on for several years, was presented at the Hofstra University Conference. It entails the use of English and ASL and involves a number of school programs. To the best of our knowledge it is the only instance we know of involving ASL instruction for which data is available. We believe this approach could provide a model for PCP. Frank Bowe, who was Chairman of the Commission on Education of the Deaf, summarized the conference with a paper entitled "Radicalism v. Reason: Directions in Educational Use of American Sign Language." He concluded that we should base our work not on rhetoric but on research, not on radicalism but on reason.

Bowe stated that the key points to come out of the conference were:

1. The field is not yet clear on its goals with respect to ASL use in the classroom.

2. We do not have good measurement tools to apply in research on ASL in the classroom.

3. We know surprisingly little about how ASL is learned by deaf children.

4. It takes years to establish an ASL program.

5. The few programs now using ASL are doing little research.

6. There is a severe shortage of ASL-fluent teachers, especially deaf educators and particularly in preschool and elementary programs, and there are few indications that teacher training programs soon will alleviate these shortages.

7. Resistance to change is strong, particularly where core beliefs about culture and language are challenged by a "bilingual/bicultural" program.

8. The research questions surrounding educational uses of ASL are so numerous, and so complex, that a long-term program of study is likely to be required for answers to be found.

In the 10/2/91 "Dean Talk" memo it is stated that the work of PCP is aligned with recommendations from the Commission on Education of the Deaf. Our reading of the position of the Chairman of the Commission, Frank Bowe, is in disagreement with your statement.

On this basis, we implore you to re-examine the methodology currently in use at PCP for implementing and assessing "no voice" and ASL-based communication strategies with deaf children in and outside the classroom. The prominence and importance of Gallaudet University's two national demonstration schools, when considered in light of the commitment to excellence articulated by President I. King Jordan at his inauguration, make it especially crucial that state-of-the-art conceptual and methodological issues be addressed throughout this new effort at PCP. To settle for less than the best may not only jeopardize the future of ASL in the education of deaf children, but also bring into serious question both the role of PCP as national demonstration models and the credibility of Gallaudet's commitment to excellence.

We propose for your consideration that an effective resolution to this need is available through the selection by PCP of qualified, impartial consultants responsible for advising your administration in the areas of curriculum development and outcomes assessment relating to ASL-based instruction. They would be able to work with your administration in assuring not only that ASL-based instruction receives a fair opportunity, but that the methodology used is indeed marked by excellence and is above scientific criticism. Given their contributions to the issues to date we believe that Professor [David] Stewart of Michigan State and Professor Bowe of Hofstra would prove to be excellent in this capacity.

[Reprinted with permission from Gallaudet University]

Gallaudet University   October 29, 1991
Department of Psychology

MEMORANDUM

TO: MSSD English Department members
FROM: Dr. Larry G. Stewart, Professor
                 Department of Psychology
SUBJECT: Response to your letter dated October 15, 1991

Thank you for sharing your perceptions regarding the decision of the Precollege Programs administration to encourage Precollege teachers to use ASL in their classrooms and related issues. I appreciate your taking the time to communicate with me, and particularly note and appreciate the tone of reason conveyed throughout your remarks. The noted therapist and author Frederick Perls once remarked, "Communication is the beginning of understanding." Within our own unique context here at Gallaudet University, these beginning efforts to communicate will hopefully lead to better understanding of one another.

I am impressed that you are all in agreement on the points listed in your letter. Please be assured that I will think very carefully of your points of view in the future.

In a recent communication to Dean Michael Deninger and KDES principal Nancy Shook from myself and Dr. Donald Moores, some of our concerns and suggestions concerning the Precollege communication practices were expressed. A copy of this communication is attached here since they are germane to the issues mentioned in your memorandum. *[this is the previous Stewart/Moores memo dated Oct. 10, 1991]*

In this response to your letter to me I will share my own perspectives so that you may better understand my

30

position with respect to communication issues in the classroom.

Public Law 94-142. The Education of All Handicapped Children Act, and subsequent regulations, mandate that each handicapped child -- including each deaf child -- receive an education based on that child's individualized needs as determined through an interdisciplinary case study.

Based on this federal requirement, if ASL were indeed to be used as the method of communication for all deaf children enrolled at MSSD and KDES, then it follows that each deaf child would have to have an IEP on file documenting that (a) an interdisciplinary case study had been completed, with a documented conclusion of the team that ASL is the means of communication most appropriate, educationally, for that child, (b) the parents were given every opportunity to participate in the IEP decision, (c) all appropriate support and other ancillary services needed by the child, including for example speech and hearing services, have been included in the IEP, and (d) specific means are in place for assessing the outcomes of these special curricular, support, and other ancillary services in the educational progression of the child. This is the law as I understand it. Consequently, my concerns for the Precollege program communication policy may be expressed through these questions:

(1) Is there a current IEP on file for the deaf children at MSSD and KDES who are affected by the decision of the Precollege Administration regarding ASL, reflecting compliance with this federal requirement? (And, since this seems to be a blanket policy, I am assuming all of the children are affected).

(2) Are there provisions in effect at MSSD and KDES for dealing with the deaf children who either are not skilled with ASL or who depend in part on speech and hearing in their communication?

(3) How are MSSD and KDES dealing with those teachers, support personnel, and other staff members who are not skilled in ASL, while at the same time proceeding with the practice of providing an ASL communication environment?

(4) How does MSSD and KDES deal with those parents and teachers and students who object to being limited to only one means of communication (in this case, ASL)?

(5) Has Precollege Programs informed the Local Education Agencies (LEA's, or the students' home school, which referred the students enrolled at MSSD and KDES as required by federal and state statute) about this decision of the Precollege Programs administration re: ASL and sign-without-voice, and, also, requested LEA approval of such educational programming consistent with the provisions of Public Law 94-142?

Empirical Evidence of the Effectiveness of ASL in English Instruction. I most certainly respect your professional opinions concerning the efficacy of ASL in achieving optimum teacher-student communication and in promoting the acquisition of English language competency. I am aware that many fine professionals such as yourself share this opinion. At the same time, I am sure you will agree, there are many other fine professionals who perceive matters differently. For example, there are proponents of other means of communication with deaf children and adults who are just as convinced and just as enthusiastic about their own beliefs as we are, including proponents of total communication, of oralism, of cued speech, of SEE 1, of SEE 2, and of Signed English. In fact, as we know, there are outstanding professionals like yourself who are every bit as convinced about the critical importance of oralism with deaf children as were the participants from all over the world in attendance at the 1880 ICED in Milan, where it was officially proclaimed that oralism was the *only* truly effective method of educating deaf children. Oralism proponents, then and today, right or wrong, were and are just as sincere, just as convinced, just as dedicated concerning their convictions about the effectiveness of the oral method as you are in your convictions and dedication concerning ASL.

Dr. Donald Moores, Dr. Ross Stuckless, and Dr. Frank Bowe and others who are recognized as world class researchers in deaf education, internationally renowned and respected, have each commented in different contexts that there is at present no conclusive empirical evidence with respect to the utility of ASL in effecting English language competency in deaf children. In brief, these authorities have noted, fundamental issues concerning ASL and English remain to be articulated and resolved before informed, reliable decisions may be made concerning instructional methods in schools with deaf children.

Research Evidence. Throughout the history of deafness in Europe, in Spain, and in the United States, for example, deaf people have been at the mercy of either zealous missionaries, teaching masters or gurus, grand educational philosophies, and/or exclusive communication methodologies - - of oralism in Germany, Spain, and England, of sign communication in France and the United States. Always, there

33

has been personal opinion and professional opinion to support and to oppose every effort, every approach, every method.

But now, in this country, in this century, in this year of 1991, we finally are experiencing a convergence of methodology issues (ASL vs. total communication), professional competence (teaching and research), and MSSD and KDES (as model demonstration schools, schools with outstanding teachers and other support personnel, with fully capable research components). Now it seems is surely the time for your personal and professional opinions and mine, as important as they are, to bow to the methods of scientific research. In this regard may I ask you:

1. Following on the heels of the precollege Programs administrative decision you spoke of, does MSSD and KDES currently have in place research plans designed to identify and assess the processes and outcomes of this new effort to use ASL exclusively in the classroom, and to use sign-without-voice by everyone?

2. Is this research plan a robust one, conforming to the highest standards of educational research in this country, and in keeping with the cornerstone of *[Gallaudet]* President I. King Jordan's administration -- excellence?

3. Have parents of the MSSD and KDES students been fully informed of the risks and benefits of the research that is being undertaken at MSSD and KDES in the use of ASL with their children, in keeping with federal statutes concerning human research? Are they supportive or resentful -- both attitudes relevant to assessment of the effectiveness of ASL in education?

4. Are all of the teachers and other personnel at MSSD and KDES supportive of the new ASL and signing-without-voice initiative, thereby assuring a fair chance to demonstrate

the utility of this language or method in the education of deaf children? Or are some of them resentful, hostile, reluctant, thereby posing the risk of sabotage to the outcomes?

Closing Comments: I must say I am impressed with your openness and sincerity in exchanging your professional views with me. This reflects well on MSSD as a member of the Gallaudet community and I thank you for being this way. At the same time, I must share with you the fact that I have been told some disturbing things that do not at all fit our high ideals. For example:

1. Some teachers and support workers at both MSSD and KDES have contacted me in recent weeks to thank me for raising questions and to tell me: (a) they were not given any choice but were told they *had to* use ASL and *were not* to use their voice, (b) they expressed fear over speaking out against the new policy (and they insist it IS a policy even if the administration won't say so.) They state further that peer pressure to conform in the use of and signing without voice is a terrible stress on them.

2. Some parents of children at Precollege Programs sent me copies of their letters to your administrators in which they stated they had NOT been told in advance of the new approach and did not want their children limited to only one communication approach. Two sets of parents went so far as to say they would ask for an investigation from the U.S. Office of Education if the new policy were not abandoned. *[Some letters from parents are on file at the Gallaudet Archives.]*

3. An administrator within Precollege Programs told me there is currently no research plan in place for evaluating the outcomes this new communication approach at MSSD.

4. Some of the information coming out of Precollege Programs administration addressed to teachers, staff, and

parents contains what appears as distorted, biased information. Dr. Donald Moores and I refer to this in our recent memorandum to Dr. Deninger and Ms. Shook. *[This is the Moores-Stewart October 10, 1991 memo.]* As an additional example, Precollege Programs referred several times, in documents disseminated to staff and parents, to the importance of ASL as contained in the Gallaudet University mission statement (i.e., embracement of a bilingual, bicultural approach which includes use of ASL). However, to my knowledge, at no time has this information included the definition of ASL that was adopted by the University Faculty on 04/30/90. This definition reads as follows:

> The term, American Sign language (ASL), is to be used in an all-inclusive sense, even including signs expressed in English word order, with or without voice -- in much the same way deaf and hard of hearing people communicate among themselves with hearing people. (see Section 2.2, University Faculty Guidelines, Communication Policy)

This definition, I might point out, is not consistent with some of the claims being made concerning ASL in certain Precollege Program documents.

In the future, as you and other responsible teachers and administrators at Precollege Programs consider crucial communication issues, I respectfully encourage you to ponder this question: If you were a faculty member at Gallaudet, as I am, would you become involved if you learned that only one method of communication -- perhaps oralism, perhaps cued speech -- would henceforth become the communication policy at MSSD (or KDES)? Or would you stay out of it?

Again, thank you for your communication with me.

[Reprinted with permission from Gallaudet University]

DEBUNKING THE BILINGUAL/ BICULTURAL SNOW JOB IN THE AMERICAN DEAF COMMUNITY

Prologue

In recent years I have been alternately amused, perplexed, mystified, and concerned by what I see as the spread of intellectual claptrap in the deaf community concerning the so-called failure of total communication and of deaf education, while at the same time exotic theories concerning bilingualism and biculturalism *[The Bi-Bi movement]* are being propagandized with little apparent thought for truth or the long-term consequences for individuals, families, and institutions. Arcane linguistic and cultural theories are being promoted concerning "the language of the deaf," "the culture of the deaf," and "the failure of deaf education," presented not as the pure speculations they are but as absolute facts to deaf people, their families, and the general public.

Assorted linguistic and cultural "groupies," clamoring worshipfully around their gurus, have been chanting and peddling such hurtful, divisive, and intellectually-bankrupt slogans as "Down with English; ASL is the natural language of all deaf people!," "Deaf people are oppressed by hearing people," and "Hearing parents are not fit to raise deaf children. We deaf adults should take over and raise them." This type of hurtful foolishness is being used to brainwash young deaf and hard-of-hearing high school and college students to conform to expectations that they will reject their English backgrounds, oral or signed, and in the process criticize their parents and former hearing teachers for not having used ASL with them. This brainwashing has even generated feelings of guilt within many deaf adults who possess effective oral and signed English skills, leading them to avoid public use of their skills but instead to use ASL in an exaggerated manner and to become militant proponents of the ASL-only philosophy. Many of our so-called deaf leaders are being taken in by this cult-like movement, some of them even getting on the bilingual/bicultural bandwagon and spreading inanities of their own. A prime recent example of this was seen at two federally-sponsored demonstration schools for deaf children *[MSSD and KDES]* which U.S. taxpayers are supporting through approximately $25 million federal appropriations each year. There, attempts were made, but finally rebuffed under Congressional pressures, to introduce and enforce an "ASL-only, voice-off" communication policy in the classroom in a manner clearly contrary to the official total communication philosophy and, more seriously, in apparent disregard for procedural safeguards provided through federal IEP regulations mandating individualized educational programming for each child.

ASL and Deaf Culture: Creations, Not Discoveries

I believe that what has come to be known today as American Sign Language (ASL) is a special variety of what was once considered simply as "sign language." Theorizing and anthropological excavations aside, pragmatic indicators suggest that sign language and its many modern-day branches and roots and twigs and sprouts developed in both natural and contrived ways among deaf persons, those who worked with them, and those who theorized about them.

It also strikes me "deaf culture" was not discovered; it was created for political purposes. The term has yet to be satisfactorily defined. Perhaps reality resists political correctness in this instance, for in too many respects to ignore, the American deaf community little resembles a cultural group as we normally consider the concept. This was documented in an unexpected manner recently in a 1991 report by the Middle States Association of Colleges and Schools on Gallaudet University:

The (accreditation) team notes that "cultural diversity" (and "multiculturalism," a term also used in the self-study) appear to have different meanings for Gallaudet University and others. For understandable reasons, the self-study stresses the status of the deaf and hard of hearing from the point of cultural distinctiveness, while noting that the group is far from monolithic. Readers of the document outside of the University, however, expect to learn more about ethnic minorities and women when they see the term "cultural diversity."

The Deaf World

Historically, deaf people have gained a more positive sense of personal identity, developed stronger feelings of self-esteem and self-confidence, and derived greater social satisfaction from congregating with one another in social activities, for civic and recreational purposes, in religious worship, and for many other purposes such as group advocacy. In the process, they did so with no need of the panache of the umbrella of "deaf culture." In recent years, however, increasing numbers of deaf people have appeared to feel the need to gather under this symbolic sanctifying umbrella.

In the larger sense of world cultures, the meaning of culture is so powerful and complex that to apply it so narrowly to a group of highly diverse deaf Americans citizens, whose members are as heterogeneous as the general population, simply makes no sense. Deaf people are scattered across the nation amidst families with ancestors from every subculture, and they are living, loving, working, and playing in the mainstream of contemporary American culture.

A Linguistic and Cultural Snow Job

It is proposed here that a linguistic and cultural snow job is being pulled on the American deaf community. The primary influences giving rise to this snow job include these: the rise, expansion, and indiscriminate marketing of prescriptive linguistics within the deaf community; the presentation and propagandization of linguistic theory as a foundation for educational methods; long-standing frustrations among deaf persons and their teachers associated with English-acquisition by prelingually deaf individuals; deep-seated resentments and hostility among many deaf people associated with the social stigmas and sequelae historically placed on deafness and sign language in our society; the painful search of deaf individuals for a place in the sun in a world where the coin of the realm is spoken language; and evolving trends in American society.

Peddlers of culture are adroit at sidestepping inconvenient details of reality that are inconsistent with their snow job. Seldom mentioned in today's ASL-only, "deaf culture," and deaf education-bashing snow job in the deaf community are the adverse effects on children from such harmful factors as high rates of divorce and family breakdown, the growing incidence of poverty and hunger, the stresses on children in remarriages, spousal abuse, child neglect and abuse, the absence of parents from the home who must work to survive, alcoholism and drug abuse, AIDS, urban and suburban violence, stresses associated with contemporary life in the midst of the breakdown of traditional religious and societal values, and the pervasive effects of the widening gaps that separate the poor, the homeless, the middle class, and the wealthy. The inconvenient fact that deaf children have been increasingly affected by these harmful elements just as much as hearing children is notably missing in the rhetoric offered by bashers of deaf education and peddlers of ASL-only as educational methodology.

Fingerpointing and Blaming

Over the past several years there has been more and more fingerpointing and blaming leveled from one quarter to another within the deaf community. ASL-users decry signed English users, and vice-versa. Those born deaf deride those who become deaf at six years or twelve years or later. ASL-users who do not use lip movements scorn those who sign with mouthed English, or, the other way around. Residential school graduates turn up their nose at mainstream graduates, or the reverse. And so it goes: a once cohesive community now splintered apart by ideology.

Recent years have appeared to introduce new strains of arrogance and irresponsibility within the deaf community. Indeed, we deaf people appear to have our share of finger-pointers and cry-babies, just as is the case in the hearing community. Some of our advocacy activities actually appear to invite new barriers between deaf people and mainstream America. Not long ago there appeared an article in an advocacy agency's newspaper, "Hearing people: Where do they fit in the deaf community." (DCARA NEWS, San Leandro, CA., August 1990, (p. 1). In it one deaf writer stated:

> My disenchantment with the majority group surfaces only when these people step in front of us and make decisions we feel are ours to make; when they attempt to dictate programs and a

dependent lifestyle for us; when they advocate for the deaf without license from us . . .

This appears as a typical perpetuation of the "us" vs. "them" mentality that is fragmenting the larger American community today. Such narrow-minded articles invite the same type of stereotyping from hearing people, perhaps in the form of such questions as "Deaf people: Where do they fit in the hearing community?"

There are other troubling shibboleths rampant in the deaf community today:

"We are NOT hearing impaired" [never mind that this term is used throughout medical science, rehabilitation, and audiology]. Note this excerpt from Gallaudet University Alumni Newsletter (Jan.-Feb., 1990):

. . . I am very disturbed by the term "hearing impaired . . . we are NOT disabled . . .

This is a clear example of "politically correct" ideology in the deaf community. The statement is simply untrue. As evidence that such slogans are essentially false and self-deceptive, it is a fact that deaf or hearing leaders of the bilingual, bicultural movement in the deaf community are never to be found protesting the classification of deaf people as "disabled" whenever federal and state government agencies hand out millions of tax dollars for program support, entitlement services programs such as Vocational Rehabilitation and Social Security Disability Insurance, special education for deaf children, higher education for deaf persons, and many more -- every one of them having eligibility criteria that include the presenceof a disability. As further evidence, the deaf community was out in full force stomping for the enactment of the Americans With Disabilities Act, and we can be sure deaf people will want to be there in the years ahead as disabled beneficiaries of ADA benefits.

In false pride or in politically-correct self-deception, some are quick to proclaim to the world, "We deaf folks are not disabled, we are not hearing-impaired!" Yet, just as quickly those same people are the first in line for disability-related benefits. .

Here are yet more "bilingual/bicultural deaf community" shibboleths:

> A capital D must be used to refer to people who are culturally deaf (as in Deaf).

This is another example of a "politically correct" response in the deaf community, where social pressure is brought to bear in forcing the semantic preferences of small special interest groups on others, preferences that are unrelated to common rules of English usage.

> "Deaf teachers do not need to pass a national test of English proficiency because such tests are discriminatory in view of the fact that the natural language of the deaf is ASL."

How on earth do we expect proper English to be learned by deaf students if there is no standard of English usage among teachers, both deaf and hearing, for both modeling and instructional purposes? Modeling is a critical aspect of language development, and to think otherwise is both foolish and inconsistent with reality. Unwise standards not only will result in the lowering of professional expectations of English competency among deaf teachers; they will also send the unfortunate, and false, message to the public that "Deaf teachers have inferior English skills." One thing we can be sure of: poor English usage on the part of the teacher, deaf or hearing, will adversely affect English competency development in deaf children.

> "ASL is able to convey the same meanings, information, and complexities as English. The mode of expression is different, but only at the delivery level . . . ASL is . . . capable of stating all the information expressed in English and of doing this within the same conceptual frame. (Hoffmeister, Robert J., 1989. ASL and its implications for education. in H. Bornstein (Ed.). Manual Communication: Implications for Education. Washington, D.C.: Gallaudet University Press, pp. 8 1-107.)

This is pure baloney. ASL, as linguistically defined, has nowhere near the power of English for receptive OR expressive purposes. ASL has its own merits, some of them outshining spoken language, but anywhere near as powerful as English for education, commerce, and all-around communication purposes it most certainly is not.

> "Only deaf people know what is best for deaf people, ergo only deaf people are qualified to speak out on issues affecting deaf people."

This is more "politically correct" talk that is pure circular poppycock. Best in what way, for what purposes? Do we need a deaf doctor to tell deaf people what is best for their indigestion? Do we need a deaf heart surgeon to decide what is best for a deaf person who is considering a by-pass? These are ultimately empty words, for they serve no purpose. But, they can be damaging words where relations between deaf and hearing people who live or work together are concerned.

> "Deaf children should be raised by deaf adults because hearing people do not understand deafness nor do they use the native language of deaf people - ASL."

ASL: SHATTERING THE MYTH

This is pure nonsense, especially in the United States of America where no group tells another group how to raise their children. Such is an insult to parents and to the U.S. Constitution. Further, it is belittling to children who are deaf to cast them always as D-E-A-F rather than as the human beings they are. Children who are deaf are children far more than they are deaf children. To propose that one's hearing status is a major determinant of one's parenting skills is an intellectually bankrupt effort. And the idea that ASL -- and not, for example, signed English -- is the natural language of deaf children in this country is pure self-serving propaganda on the part of a very small group of people on a power trip.

"Deaf people are oppressed by hearing people."

Deaf people oppressed? By hearing people? Webster's dictionary says "oppress" means, first, to suppress or "to crush or burden by abuse of power or authority." Or, two, "to burden spiritually or mentally as if by pressure." Through ignorance and sometimes insensitivity, some hearing people do treat deaf people badly at times. These same hearing people also treat other hearing people badly. All in all, considering everything this country is doing for deaf people, anyone who says deaf people here are being oppressed, and by hearing people, needs serious attitude adjustment. Such an adjustment would occur instantly through a weeks' stay in some country like Iraq or Cuba, where they would learn a new definition of "oppression."

A Point of View

Most knowledgeable professionals in the field of deafness acknowledge and appreciate the value of sign language. However, as we penetrate through the snow that is currently enveloping the American deaf community, there should be no doubt in anyone's mind that the bilingualism/biculturalism movement has the singular goal of making ASL, which means ASL-only and no use of voice, the method of classroom instruction for all deaf children. While a stated subsidiary goal of the movement may be to teach English, as is claimed, this will effectively turn English into a second language (ESL) for deaf Americans who were born in this country. The peddlers of this concept downplay this reversal in priorities by riding on the intellectual coattails of the broader bilingual/bicultural movement, *[To wit: the compulsory placement of children in classes where all the instruction is in Spanish, for no better reason than that the child's parents are immigrants, or merely because of a Spanish surname, even children whose sole language is English.]* which has effectively legitimized the teaching of English as a second language even to born-in-America citizens from a variety of ethnic groups.

Today, our world is far too complex and demanding, and we simply no longer can afford needless "us" vs. "them" feelings that serve to splinter the community -- ASL-proponents vs. Signed English proponents, deaf people vs. hard-of-hearing people, deaf people vs. other disabled people, or deaf people vs. hearing people.

We need to wake up and see snow jobs for what they are: illusions. Turning away from the larger community and creating a world of our own -- especially a world that we expect taxpayers to subsidize -- is not only an unwise answer for the deaf community, it will ultimately prove to be a self-destructive one.

Within the deaf community it is time for us to set aside the separatism that today divides us over language issues and issues of identity and self-esteem. We are all, hearing and deaf alike, worthy human beings. None of us should feel the need to gather under a cultural umbrella based on untruths in order to obtain feelings of belonging and identity. While respecting the languages and cultures of others, as Americans it is our responsibility, and our duty, to maintain as our first culture the American culture, and as our first language the English language. If we must fight to gain full acceptance within American culture, or struggle to help deaf children attain English competence, then let us fight and struggle, just as others have done in this country. There is, after all, no free lunch -- no matter what a snow job may claim.

[This essay has been condensed from the original version which was published in "Viewpoints on Deafness, A Deaf American Monograph" (Vol. 42, 1992). Reprinted with permission from the National Association of the Deaf. "Viewpoints on Deafness" can be ordered from the NAD.]

CHAPTER TWO

THE ESSAYS OF
FRANCES M. PARSONS

WHY ASL?

An uproar about ASL has burst out at several places involved with the education of the deaf at the university, high school and middle school levels. Recently two middle school pupils verbally attacked a teacher and a staff member for their failure to use ASL and for "discriminating" against the deaf. Who was responsible for brainwashing those kids? As much as I want to be brief, my years of experience compel this lengthy response.

As a prelingually and congenitally deaf person born to hearing parents, I learned ASL from my school peers while learning English-based signs with speech from my teachers and houseparents, so I feel that I have the right to speak out. I do admire some ASL linguists *[There is a growing concern that the difference between linguists who study voice or spoken language and those who study signs or manual com-munications be clearly defined when the term "linguists" is used. It has also been said that "manual communication linguists" is the correct term for those studying signs, not "ASL linguists."]* and deaf friends but am crestfallen to see them so aggressive and spiteful against all forms of sign

48

language, (in particular, signs based on English or used in English-word-order) except ASL, which they glorify. Some throw me dagger looks or curse me. Every time I oppose ASL as the ultimate answer, as the best means of education, I am reprimanded and told not to speak out against ASL. I have been warned that I would end up as the number one enemy of deafdom. I would be an outcast, I would forever regret what I had done, et cetera.

I have survived die-hard oralists' literally throwing rotten eggs at me, walking out of auditoriums where I was speaking, or shutting their school doors in my face during my 1974, '76 and '77 global tours when I campaigned for Total Communication, a method of utilizing English-word-order signing and speech at the same time.

Controversy about ASL rages ad infinitum. Pros and cons. Contempt vs. idolization. Should ASL be the recommended language for classrooms in kindergartens, elementary schools, high schools, colleges and the university? Should ASL be the required language for higher learning? Should people be required to know both English and ASL? By this I am referring to the Bi-Bi method of educating the deaf which teaches the deaf child ASL first, then after fluency is attained, the child is taught English as a second language. Speech is taught much later, if at all. *[As Stewart brought up previously, there is no evidence that Bi-Bi works. In fact, "Bilingual-Bicultural" probably is incorrect (and certainly confusing) terminology as the emphasis is on ASL with English of only secondary importance, certainly not both, in the literal sense of the word.]* It seems to me that there is a strong resemblance between the negative attitudes of the diehard oralists, in particular, those who oppose any use of sign language, and those of many diehard ASLists. Some of

49

these oralists have an ironclad demand for the deaf to speak as normally as possible, and fly into a rage when the deaf either fail to speak or want to use sign language. Now, the ASLists use the same approach when the hearing fail to learn ASL, or if they choose to use signs based on English or signs in English word order. You, the deaf, *know* it's impossible for most deaf people to speak as perfectly as the oralists want. So please, please, do not expect the hearing to meet your demand to use fluent signs, especially ASL.

For years, living in the world of the hearing, I have endured the oralists' expecting me to accept their terms. One day as I was signing to a deaf person in a room full of hearing people, a British principal turned toward me and lashed out for all to hear: "Use your voice so we can hear what you're saying. You are cutting us out." I replied: "You use sign language so we the deaf can understand what you're saying. We the deaf have *always* been cut out." Every hearing person, a parent, a friend, a nurse, a teacher, a staff member, a lawyer, etc., who tries his or her best to sign for the sake of communicating with us, who goes out of his or her way to learn to sign, is a living jewel. Even those who sign badly should be appreciated and encouraged, not condemned or criticized because of their inability to sign fluently.

At an alarming rate, the hearing professionals working with the deaf are becoming frustrated, discouraged and fearful of losing their positions because of the increasingly strident demands of some deaf "leaders," as well as a number of hearing leaders, who have insisted ASL usage be mandatory. Some hearing teachers, staff members and interpreters, who have taken time, effort, expense and trouble to take courses in special education and learn sign language only to be sabotaged by the recent mandatory requirements to use ASL, exclusively, have begun to withdraw from their studies or resign from their jobs. If this momentum continues to accelerate, there will be a dearth of highly qualified hearing professionals working with or for the deaf. The deaf may then find themselves isolated in a small circle with little access to hearing society.

Many interpreters already find their jobs thankless, underpaid, without health benefits, and they are expected to work in conditions detrimental to safety and well-being. Yet they are condemned, the victims of hatred and abuse from those deaf who practice "deafism." *[These people are often described as ASLists, deaf militants or deaf radicals]* No wonder there is an increasing shortage of good and dedicated interpreters.

This ASL controversy, with its accompanying unhealthy antagonism, is deepening the chasm between the deaf and the hearing. It seems ironic to me how they consider themselves as a minority group and ask to be recognized and seek financial support in order to retain their culture status; yet they lash out at the world of the majority, creating havoc along the way.

Research findings by ASL supporters may not be correct. I have to question the validity and reliability of *some* of these deaf education or deaf studies dissertations and research work, based on my own experience. Researchers studying for their Ph.D.'s often had research questions that were vague or garbled. When asked for clarification, they would say, "Never mind, just answer as best as you can." Some of my colleagues even advised me to answer randomly just to please them. Others have told me, "I don't understand the questions, but I don't care what I answered because I got paid."

In contrast, Dr. Donald F. Moores' *[A highly regarded researcher at Gallaudet]* past and present statistical reports can be regarded as realistic because they are based on objective evidence and findings resulting from deaf pupils' use of the Total Communication method. In fact, I have highly recommended his books worldwide.

During the early years of Gallaudet in the 19th century, peace reigned as the students and faculty used sign language based largely on English. It stemmed from Laurent Clerc who taught signs to educators of the deaf in proper English-word-order along with a considerable amount of fingerspelling.

Laurent Clerc, a deaf man from France, was persuaded to come to the United States and teach his signs to deaf Americans, by Thomas Hopkins Gallaudet, who went to Europe in 1815 seeking new ways of reversing the woeful educational conditions of the deaf here at that time. After being unable to work something out with the British, he went to France where he eventually met up with Clerc. Clerc obtained his knowledge of these signs, often referred to as the "manual or methodical signs," from the famous French educator of the deaf, the Abbe de l'Epee.

Laurent Clerc's classic signs in English-word-order is the *true* legacy and heritage the Gallaudet alumni have for so long passed down to deaf pupils all over the United States until recent years. The more intelligent the deaf were, the more they fingerspelled. Fingerspelling is used to spell out a word in the case a term does not have a sign. The less intelligent (or educated) a deaf person was, the less tendency there was to fingerspell.

Clerc's heritage began to fall apart after the infamous Milan Conference in 1880 which banned the use of sign language in classrooms. As many schools converted to oralism, deaf students began to use sign language only among themselves in the dorms, and adherence to English-word-order fell out of favor resulting in what is known as ASL today.

Recently, heated arguments about ASL have accelerated tenfold destroying what little was left of Clerc's signs. Isn't it ironic that so many propose to rename our university *[Gallaudet]* after Clerc, who, if he knew that today's ASL (which still consists of some of his signs, but not in English-word-order) was to be mandatory at Gallaudet, would be literally "whirling in his grave."

It has been brought up by some that deaf children of deaf adults (DOD) have a better command of English. They attributed that to ASL and began to glorify it. During those 21 years when I was teaching at Gallaudet, I observed the changing attitudes of the students who became more apathetic and demanded easier exams and more ASL. Many couldn't read fingerspelling. In my early years of teaching I used mostly English-word-order signing, with dashes of ASL to grip their attention. In my last few years I was asked to use more ASL. Too often, many failed to understand the words I fingerspelled and I had to reduce my language usage to the lowest level (or to the highest level, as defined by the ASLists) of ASL to get the concept through. With a little "hunting," I found numerous students with such a weak command of English, I couldn't fathom how they had been admitted to Gallaudet in the first place. Later, I was stunned to learn that some of these former students who never learned to write became teachers! Deaf children of deaf adults have good English skills? Not that I witnessed during my years as a teacher.

Questioning students with a good command of English, I found that their English skills were attributed *mostly to reading*. So libraries, chock-full of books, are indeed our best friends and educators.

ASL: SHATTERING THE MYTH

I do welcome ASL as a means of communication outside the classrooms, but for all educational-use communication, signing *must* be based on the language of the larger mainstream society if we expect our deaf children to succeed in today's world.

[Submitted by Frances M. Parsons. Condensed and revised from an earlier version which was printed in the June 1990 issue of Silent News]

THE DARK SIDE OF BI-BI

For some time now a "natural language of the deaf" (ASL) awareness has gained momentum. Then the Bilingual-Bicultural (Bi-Bi) ideology emerged along with the claim of being the ultimate answer for the education of the deaf. However, I had very little idea about the actual driving motives behind the Bi-Bi approach until I was invited to give a presentation at a certain residential school for the deaf.

During the three-day visit to that school, I was overwhelmed by many hearing teachers who eagerly invited me to visit their classes -- in fact, their friendly pupils were encouraged to write me lovely thank you letters for my presentation which included enthusiastically encouraging more reading. I was speechless to get such a positive reaction from so many students.

Just as I have at many other schools that I have visited all over the United States, I tremendously enjoyed giving presentations and pep talks to the growing generation of these young deaf. Many were inspired and later came to Gallaudet to pursue higher learning and others joined the Peace Corps or traveled overseas. I was pleased and surprised when they approached me to say "Thank you!"

Yet there is a dark side, a hype and a thorn in the rose side to the Bi-Bi approach. I brought a copy of *"Why ASL?"* *[the preceding essay in this book]* that had already been widely circulated on the Gallaudet campus, merely to share it with a certain friend. It was so admired that more copies were made -- and distributed. Then all hell broke loose. I was reprimanded by an assistant superintendent after a certain deaf teacher and Bi-Bi Coordinator raised an objection after being displeased with the essay. In fact, the assistant principal, who did not read the essay, *supervised* my talk with the teachers at the library -- KGB style with complete disregard for the Bill of Rights!

Later, after presenting seven different talks in classes and in the auditorium, using my ASL quite generously, I squeezed in a few moments to ask a bunch of middle school pupils if they would please have patience for some of the hearing who were not fluent in ASL, after I noticed these pupils were making rude remarks about them. Result? A deaf teacher personally rebuked me for my remark explaining that because of *her* bad experience with the hearing, (mostly speech therapists, audiologists and some hearing teachers) *the young deaf of this generation are to be protected!* Her kind of remarks have been repeated by numerous other deaf adults. Later, I received very negative letters from two middle school teachers, and several critical letters from the middle school kids who were apparently incited and coached by one of those teachers! *[These letters are on file at the Gallaudet University Archives]* I have been treated more courteously by die-hard oralists than by some of these Bi-Bi extremists!

These incidents, along with a number of other things, have me questioning the credibility of a Bi-Bi program. This method appears one-sided and seems to overprotect deaf children to the point of breeding hatred towards the hearing world. An eight-year-old deaf child already complained that he wished his mama was deaf because she cannot use fluent ASL. My parents, my children, my relatives and many of my wonderful friends are hearing so I cannot stomach the stormy, emotional, trend of "protecting," which appears to be a by-product of this aggressive Bi-Bi approach.

During my early childhood years, I experienced nasty clashes in my speech training -- in fact, one teacher harangued me to pronounce "P" until I was blue in the face and spat at her. I was dismissed from oral school and went to the California School for the Deaf at Berkeley. My bad experience in the oral method did not cause me to resent all hearing people.

I do not believe that Total Communication, English-word-order signing or even oralism is the cause for the failure of deaf children to learn English, nor can I believe that ASL is the final savior for these problems. There is evidence from old compositions written by Gallaudet and deaf school students in the 19th century that their English was good -- and those students used Clerc's signs in English-word-order.

I strongly support deaf teachers as role models, but I cannot support the attempt by deaf adults to instigate young deaf children to *demand* respect from the hearing while they themselves live in a world full of social and moral shortcomings!

I have believed for a long time that while deaf children of deaf parents have admirable leadership qualities, not so admirable is the tendency to impose their wishes on the deaf from hearing families, and the hearing *[quite a few advocates for the Bi-Bi method are deaf of deaf or "DOD"].*

For a long time, Gallaudet has been a Mecca for the deaf nationally and internationally. But now that Gallaudet has

56

seemed to embrace ASL and Bi-Bi, many foreign educators are leery, not happy with this present trend. However, a large number of the Gallaudet faculty members may in fact not agree with the ASL advocates (that have seemed to dominate things politically) but have chosen for the most part to remain silent rather than have to deal politically with the aggressive stance of these ASL advocates.

The Bi-Bi approach comes with a lot of excess baggage and many Bi-Bi proponents are quite vague in their own understanding of it. A main component, using ASL to teach deaf children English, has never been proven to work. If Bi-Bi actually does work, then it will be quite clear and obvious to everybody. So far, this remains to be seen. In the meantime we have produced another generation of deaf children that still can't read and write.

[Submitted by Frances M. Parsons. Condensed and revised from an earlier version which was printed in the Sept. 1990 issue of The DCARA News]

MEMORANDUM

To: Gallaudet University Faculty
From: Frances M. Parsons, Associate Professor
Date: 2 November 1992
RE: ASL In Schools

The recent conference concerning "ASL In Schools: Policies and Curriculum" was disappointing and did not reflect the diverse views of ASL in the deaf community today.

A broader representation of ASL was what I expected to reap from this conference, not the restrictive approach which was presented. I had proposed at an earlier faculty meeting a system of signs in English-word-order, with or without voice, speechreading, and with moderate facial and body expressions. English-based signs in English-word-order is already used by the majority of sign language users who are, by and large, found in mainstream settings. This proposal provides a logical compromise for all social and educational levels of the deaf. I noticed at the conference many of the proponents of ASL actually signed in English-word-order among themselves.

Why not read Larry Stewart's "Debunking the Bilingual/Bicultural Snow Job in the American Deaf Community"? It is only one of many highly articulate and representative expressions that opposes the ASL and Bilingual-Bicultural ideologies.

One of the militant extremists had set an example of how they *terrorize* anyone who opposes ASL, Deaf Culture or Deaf Studies by sending me this unsigned letter which ridiculed my support for English and English-based signing:

THE INTERNATIONAL LEAGUE OF DEAF PARANOIDS
is pleased to announce that
THE DELUDED DEAF PERSON OF THE YEAR AWARD
goes to
FRANCIS M. PARSONS
It is further pleased to announce that
THE HEARING ***-KISSER OF THE YEAR AWARD
also goes to
FRANCIS M. PARSONS

THIS AWARD IS GIVEN IN RECOGNITION OF HER
OUTSTANDING WORK:

1.   As an ugly American who has created total communication chaos among Deaf people in many countries by forcing Deaf children to use English-word-order signs instead of native sign languages.
2.   As an ugly Gallaudetian who has spread misinformation and lies about the bilingual-bicultural movement in America.
3.   As an ugly DOHA *[deaf of hearing adult]* who has tried to divide and conquer Deaf people by polarizing them between those with Deaf parents and those with hearing parents.

4.   As an ugly human being who has unleashed her terrible venom and attacked anyone who opposes her point of view.

5.   As an ugly Uncle Tom who has always supported the hearing point of view and never that of the Deaf.

6.   As an ugly English user who has spread lies about ASL, one of the most beautiful and expressive languages in America. In recognition of her outstanding work we have awarded her A FREE ONE-WAY TICKET TO ST. ELIZABETH'S HOSPITAL

Oh Please, St. E., Just set us free, of Frances P.
Please post this announcement all over Gallaudet

TO: FM Parsons
FROM: LG Stewart
SUBJ: Hang in there.

Peggy, I'm sorry that you had to receive that hateful letter.

The sad thing is that the writer(s) is/are clearly intelligent. That they use their abilities in such a hateful, cowardly way is a tragedy.

Hold your head up high. Time will take care of things.

Larry

TO: LGStewart
FROM: FMParsons
SUBJ: Not giving up!

I am distributing hundreds of copies of this anonymous letter all over the Gallaudet campus, just to show how cowardly that person is and as a classic example of how the extremists use their tactics to intimidate those who oppose ASL.

Peggie.

ASL: SHATTERING THE MYTH

[Both Stewart and Parsons were subject to hate mail, character assassination, verbal harassment, and for Parsons, physical assault for disagreeing with some of the militant supporters of ASL and deaf culture. However, they did have many on- and off-campus supporters. These are a few written comments that they have received and are on file at the Gallaudet University Archives.]

Peggy,

Thank you for continuing to speak out. I am truly disappointed (actually fed up is a better way of saying it) with the atmosphere here *[Gallaudet]* and am planning to leave. In many ways I feel like I am abandoning a sinking ship. That hurts me, but I cannot see why I should stay around and drown.

(Signed by a professor at Gallaudet)

Peggy,

Thank you for sharing your distressing, good thoughts about Gally, ASL, Militantism, etc. Of course I do not have the same depth and breadth of your experiences but I can agree with you. I can't help being hearing, and I don't like being blamed for it, condemned automatically. But I know better than to say anything publicly.

(Signed by a member of the Gallaudet faculty)

[Condensed and updated from material submitted by Frances M. Parsons]

SHATTERING THE MYTH

When the ASL-as-a-language movement emerged in the 70's I was a stanch supporter! I attended ASL workshops, retreats, classes or presentations until I began to notice a disturbing trend: English was to be condemned, downgraded, shunned and relegated to second fiddle. Speech was almost never mentioned. ASL *militancy* began to grow by leaps and bounds. Then I began to oppose this ideology. Not sign language itself, but the insistence that signs *not* be used in English-word-order.

My opposition to usage of ASL in the educational setting enraged ASL supporters. These linguists, sign language researchers, deaf studies instructors, and so on, struck back. I was forbidden to ask questions at presentations, banished from the platform at ASL conferences and meetings. In short, I was treated like a leper.

A number of English supporters tried to work out a compromise diplomatically, even suggesting keeping the ASL signs, but used in a fairly consistent correct English order. But the ASL movement has a rigid, no compromise platform. With the Gallaudet University enrollment smaller these days, I strongly urged for wider choices in communications as well as working with mainstream and hard-of-hearing organizations to help ensure the university survives. This is apparently not a concern for the ASL supporters.

I find it very absurd that proponents of ASL have a mandate that ASL be taught with a *specific* facial expression for each sign. In addition, they are studying written ASL. (Which word future me know hard give up habit-old me.) This has to be one of the most primitive and backward approaches in education ever thrust upon the deaf, and the hearing!

Deaf of deaf *[deaf children who have deaf parents, usually from the deaf community]* educators are saying: "We deaf of deaf families are qualified to decide what is best for all deaf children (especially those with hearing parents) on education, deaf culture, Bi-Bi, and ASL." Where does that leave us deaf people who have hearing parents? Are we "not qualified" to speak out?

61

ASL: SHATTERING THE MYTH

Leaders of the deaf overseas are thoroughly disgusted with these American ASL linguists (both hearing and deaf) who use their ASL research grants to travel overseas to *command* them to use ASL and disregard signs based on English or in English-word-order in their deaf educational programs. These researchers wreak havoc by turning deaf against deaf, and especially, the deaf against the hearing. Many in France, Sweden and Finland think *everybody* in America is in favor of ASL over English-based signing. Nothing is farther from the truth.

These overseas deaf leaders look to knowledge of English as the key to success in their countries. Many of the successful deaf programs are based on English signing, and yet these deaf militants from America were downplaying the value of English, attempting to "rescue" deaf children from their hearing parents by claiming to know what is best for them. They have left behind a trail of broken dreams, strained relationships and unemployable deaf students without mastery of English, all for the sake of preservation of ASL.

These militants see no wrongdoing in upsetting a delicate balance reached by educators in some mainstreaming settings, by ordering the students not to speak, but to sign only -- preferably in ASL. Mainstreamed or orally-educated deaf adults are told not to speak. Hard-of-hearing adults living in the deaf community use ASL-only out of fear. I have been rebuked many times for speaking and been considered a hearing-minded snob.

At a summer camp for deaf children, I witnessed a camp director, who was also an active ASL advocate, do a magnificent job of running the month-long program only to ruin it on the last night when she let her bias cloud her judgment and told the deaf children to return to their schools and *demand* ASL and the Bi-Bi approach be implemented.

I am quite astounded when I see these same militants signing among themselves in English-word-order, teaching their own deaf children to sign in English, with some even encouraging the use of voice, and often sending them to special programs, some with extensive oral programs -- but rarely to a residential school for the deaf. One of Gallaudet's top administrators has three deaf children who not only learned to *talk* and sign in English while being raised as children but later went on to esteemed careers rarely reached by deaf children raised solely on ASL. Yet, this Gallaudet administrator is one of the most vocal pro-ASL activists today. If this is not a classic case of hypocrisy, I don't know what is. One should practice what one preaches. She does have a dilemma: An ASL-only education isn't good enough for her own children, but the continual existence of ASL is a critical component in her family's well-being and way of life!

I remember the distinguished educator of the deaf, Edward Scouten, saying at a convention in Baltimore once: "ASL is quite undemanding intellectually; it serves as a simple and quick mode of communication for deaf children. Deaf children cannot come to grips with the hearing world if they cannot read or write in their own national language."

I strongly feel the key to a deaf child's success is parental attention and encouragement, whether deaf or hearing, to read, read, read. Go into many homes of residential school for the deaf grads and you will find it devoid of books! Survivors of residential schools who have succeeded in the mainstream world will tell you it was reading that saved them. It was true for me. Early exposure and encouragement can make all the difference.

ASL: SHATTERING THE MYTH

At Gallaudet, two English professors did intensive research on deaf students who had an excellent command of English. They consistently found, among other things, mothers who communicated constantly and voracious book reading! I only hope these professors publish their findings someday. Non-ASL research money is hard to come by, so English supporters do not have the luxury enjoyed by ASL linguists.

In speaking out for what I believe in, I have been steamrollered, stamped on, sqashed, and physically abused. I have received rude letters from grade school children encouraged by their pro-ASL teachers. My character has been falsely tarnished, flyers sent all over Gallaudet's campus ridiculing my support for English and English-based signing. My last book, "I Didn't Hear the Dragon Roar," *[a highly-acclaimed account of her solo journey throughout China]* was subject to a massive boycott initiated by these militants.

On his deathbed, dying from cancer, the late Larry Stewart urged me to carry on the fight against the ASL militants. Later, after his funeral, a deaf school teacher who was a militant supporter of ASL said right to my face: (and knowing that I was also afflicted with cancer) "hurry, you die next!"

A Gallaudet professor, one holding a PhD, was so enraged that I steadfastly stood for my principles during a faculty-student meeting at Gallaudet, that she turned and physically assaulted me by striking me from behind on the neck. My car was also vandalized and I continued to receive threats. But nothing will reduce me to a gibbering goon!

By contrast, in the early 70's, I made numerous trips abroad encouraging the use of sign language in deaf schools and spreading the word of opportunities for the deaf at

Gallaudet. I was snubbed and snarled at by many oral-method educators who walked out of the auditoriums. Many boycotted my presentations. One die-hard oral advocate sabotaged my lecture to teachers by switching off the auditorium lights in the middle of it. Yet there were many dedicated teachers who cared and were concerned that somehow strict oralism failed those deaf children. So they welcomed me, some with doubt, some with faith. The myth that signing prevented learning speech was shattered. Teachers were amazed how quickly these deaf children learned. Seeds were sown. Many of these deaf children later went to Gallaudet and into successful careers; others returned to their homelands to educate deaf children. This was repeated throughout other countries as I continued to travel globally spreading the word of sign language and Gallaudet.

In 1976 in Africa, I was kidnapped, dragged into a narrow alley and brutally thrown onto the cobblestones. This was the same part of Africa where missionaries were forced to watch their wives raped and babies heads bashed in. My assailants were three mean-looking young men with tribal scars on their faces and hatred in their eyes. One held a knife pressed against my stomach while he talked to me. I pointed my finger to my ear indicating my deafness. Only because he had a deaf sister was I spared from rape and perhaps, murder. In fact, he knelt down, kissed my hand, said I was a saint and told me to carry on my work. I have done so ever since, encouraging the usage of sign language in English-word-order. It was an Indian astrologer who once told me: "You have name and fame abroad, but you are not recognized in your homeland."

Later, I retold this incident to an African school principal. I told him how I was a coward for heading back to the hotel and crying for two hours out of sheer fright. The principal exclaimed: "You coward? How come you stayed in Africa for another month instead of flying home?"

Decades later, I returned to some of these places. Many retained the signing in proper language order methods. But I was quite disturbed to discover that, at a few places, after being visited by some "meddlesome" ASL linguists who "goaded" them into using "natural signs" (ASL) without speech, some decided to simply renounce *any* signing and revert to oralism.

Recent surveys shown to me on my last visit show schools that retained English-based signing incorporated during my 1976 global tour had student enrollment increase more than tenfold. Graduates of these progams passed exams to hearing colleges and universities, and many went on to high-position employment. These graduates do mention how they are ridiculed, snubbed and "downgraded" by ASL militants for using English-based signing instead of the "natural" language of the deaf, ASL. They feel these militants just can't accept the fact that English-based signing can result in a successful educational outcome. Most foreigners do not agree one must learn ASL first in order to learn English.

Recently in Singapore, an ASL-militant graduate of Gallaudet returned to his homeland and stirred up a hornet's nest which resulted in splitting a large national association of the deaf apart. The leader resigned, distressed to see his years of hard work gone. Then one day he received a copy of a new book titled: "A Child Sacrificed to the Deaf Culture." *[ISBN: 0-9637813-4-0]* He was thunderstruck to realize the same thing was happening in America, and not everybody agreed with these militants! He showed the book to association members and teachers and they were stunned to see how a product of Gallaudet destroyed them. They went into action, banded together, threw that militant out and restored harmony! My friends in Singapore and throughout the world now eagerly await the publication of this new book to help stop the spread of deaf militancy throughout the world. ASL is not the be-all or end-all solution to the problems of deaf education. By all indications, it appears an ASL-only education, or the closely-related cousin, the Bi-Bi approach, serves as a means to preserve a lifestyle for a select few, at the expense of creating hearing impaired children who can't read and write or talk.

Laurent Clerc's legacy is: Abbe de l 'Eppe's signs in English-word-order. Those seeking the truth won't be fooled by the hype and myths surrounding ASL.

(This essay was based on material submitted by Frances M. Parsons)

CHAPTER THREE

THE VISON THING
by Truman W. Stelle

[Dr. Stelle is currently a professor of English, and has been a member of the faculty at Gallaudet for nearly 3 decades.]

To: President's Office   October 1992
CC: Members of the English Department, Faculty
           Senate, The Deans and other favored persons
From: Truman Stelle
Subject: The vision thing [1]

You asked for our visions of Gallaudet. Mine, admittedly utopian, is of a place where truth is valued over promotional slogans, slogans which become Big Lies. A Big Lie is a public utterance, false at its core, which contains enough superficial truth, *and in whose acceptance people are sufficiently invested,* that it becomes a truism, a basic assumption, an operating principle. Increasingly over my twenty-four-year association with it, Gallaudet has been pushing Big Lies, either explicitly in the public statements of its spokespersons or implicitly in the very fabric of the way it operates. I have no high hopes that Gallaudet will break its addiction to these big lies, admitting publicly and insistently that they have been and continue to be false. Two and a half decades have made me cynical and dispirited, skeptical of protestations that honesty will ever become administration policy. Nevertheless, I deeply believe that until these false assumptions are publicly repudiated, Gallaudet will continue to be stymied by its own propaganda. [2]

BIG LIES

B.L. #1 Deaf people can do anything except hear. [3]

Examples can be cited of deaf persons who excel in virtually every career choice. The numbers who reach certain of those choices, however, and the circumstances by which they do so lead me to conclude that these options are not at this time viable for significant numbers of prelingually deaf people or even for significant numbers of Gallaudet students.

B.L. #2 Being deaf has no significant negative repercussions on a person's life. [4]

Corollary to B.L. #1. Except for organic brain disorders (mental retardation, autism, stroke, etc.), pre-lingual deafness is probably the disability most predictive of serious life-long deficiency in learning the language of one's majority culture. I take it as axiomatic that a language deficient person is cut off from the culture of the group which speaks that language. This makes deafness a disability which commonly isolates one from one's majority culture. Even if this were the only effect of prelingual deafness, its negative impact on the total person would be astounding.

B.L. #3 Gallaudet faculty members who choose in their professional roles to sign without speaking are simply making an allowable cultural/political/philosophic choice, neither more nor less responsible than choosing to sign and speak simultaneously. [5]

By extending offers of admission to potential students, a university establishes an expectation that its agents will make reasonable efforts to communicate in ways accessible to the greatest possible number of those students. Students and faculty come to Gallaudet at every point along the continuum from virtually perfect to virtually non-existent receptive skills in both spoken English and sign. Faculty members who sign without speaking exclude from access to their communication those who depend for understanding on a speech component, just as surely as those who speak without signing exclude those who depend for understanding on a signed component. To pretend that either of these choices is a responsible one at Gallaudet is to be willfully negligent.

B.L. #4 Students with the educational deficits typical of many entering Gallaudet freshmen can be raised to an acceptable approximation of a "bachelor's level" in four years, the same time required by institutions for which basic literacy is an entrance requirement. [6]

Entering Gallaudet students are not screened with the SAT, the standard assessor of ability to do college work; the reason they are not is that, except for the very best applicants, they *tend* to do so poorly on it that it fails to discriminate between those we want to accept and those we don't. The burden of proof -- that such students can catch up in four years -- is with advocates for the affirmative. If such a claim is made, I'd respond with a challenge that we test it; let us, as we once did, require all seniors to take the Graduate Record Examination or some other standardized instrument. This would allow us to compare our students with their peers nationwide. I grant that the GRE would not be ideal for this purpose -- it would compare all our seniors with *only those*

70

hoping to go on to graduate school from other colleges -- but it would give us some idea of how we're doing. At present, access to this kind of knowledge seems to be something we very carefully avoid.

B.L. #5 To declare, to students who are eager for reassurance that they really are getting a bona fide education at Gallaudet and to a public which is naive about deafness and about Gallaudet, that academic excellence is a meaningful institutional goal here is intellectually honest. 7

Many (most?) entering Gallaudet students have pervasive weaknesses in reading, writing, and computing skills and a pervasive ignorance of the cultural information one should be able to assume in a university student. This Big Lie is self-evidently false. Excellence in a university clearly requires students who are adequately prepared to do excellent work as well as teachers who are masters of both their disciplines and their craft (teaching). To call Gallaudet an excellent university is to enter the world of *Bill and Ted's Excellent Adventure.* Party on, Dude!

B.L. #6 Students with the kind and severity of reading/ writing deficits which are manifest in a large proportion of Gallaudet students can, at the same time that they are struggling to remedy those deficits, learn at a "college level" in their other courses. 8

"College level" courses typically carry an expectation that most of the specific information will be acquired outside the classroom, when solitary student confronts assigned and recommended readings. For students with the literacy deficits shared by many of Gallaudet's students, such solitary acquisition of knowledge through reading is out of the question. No professor, however gifted or dedicated, can make up for a general inability of students to acquire information through reading. And even if a professor could achieve such a feat, doing so would make her students dependent on her for their learning. A "college educated" person is generally understood to be one who knows how to learn independently, not one who knows a lot of facts but who is almost totally dependent on someone else for finding, interpreting, evaluating, etc. those facts.

B.L #7 The quality of life of a deaf person who socializes almost exclusively with other deaf persons, who is educated in schools especially for deaf persons, and whose career is in the field of deafness will be manifestly superior to the quality of life of a deaf person who achieves success independent of institutions for the deaf and of the society of other deaf people.[9] (See the book review by *[Gallaudet President]* I.K.J., Washington Post, May or June of 1991.)

Life consists of choices. The opportunities available at an institution like Gallaudet are clearly not identical to those at a university whose special mission is unrelated to any disability. I agree that Gallaudet does offer a deaf student some important advantages over a University of Chicago or a Towson State University, but to argue that these institutions have no significant advantages of their own, or that choosing one of them over Gallaudet would somehow diminish a deaf person's prospects for happiness and success, is to believe three impossible things before breakfast. To argue such a notion *publicly* is to encourage the public to think of this institution as seriously wacky. To actually believe such a notion is to *be* seriously wacky.

B.L. #8 Faculty members, the institutional rubber which meets the road, are less likely than administrators to suggest workable solutions to Gallaudet's problems. [10]

This flies in the face of the whole "quality revolution," which has shown repeatedly that those who best know their institutions' problems and who suggest the best solutions to those problems are precisely the on-line workers, not the managers and administrators.

B.L. #9 Gallaudet's Big Lies are the sole responsibility of the administration. [11]

Clearly the faculty is complicit. We are the ones who semester after semester pass students many of whom clearly cannot read our texts and many of whose tests and papers are either unreadable or patently nonsensical. Nevertheless, another of the findings of the Demming quality revolution is that institutional change toward true quality must begin at the top. Until management (the administration) models and rewards honesty, nothing will happen. I do not wish to excuse the faculty from its responsibility, but I believe that if a change toward honesty is to occur it is simply a fact of life that it will have to be the administration which takes the initiative, and then the administration will have to convince the faculty -- which cannot remember being dealt with honestly -- that it is serious. _____

I recognize that this statement makes me vulnerable to charges of political incorrectness and probably of negativism. I accept the charge of being politically incorrect. In fact I relish it, since the alternative seems to be the promotion of half-truths and outright lies.

ASL: SHATTERING THE MYTH

I deny, however, the charge of negativism; I do not choose to believe that it is negative to wish Gallaudet would tell the truth so it could stop fighting itself, ignoring what needs to be done in order to nurture its public myths and keep up appearances. To use an overworked metaphor, Gallaudet is a dysfunctional community, a community with a dirty little secret, 12 a secret of which most members are aware (at various levels of consciousness) but which the system, the community as a whole, is intent on keeping from the rest of the world. In order to keep our secrets hidden, we must act in ways which are counterproductive of the solutions to our problems. Until we face who we are 13 and admit publicly to our self-knowledge, we will be unable to make any progress that transcends the cosmetic. 14

(1) You will note that I have violated your guidelines on length. I reject the sound-bite mentality that meaningful ideas can be expressed in one sentence. It reminds me of students who believe they can meaningfully answer a question about the structure of a novel in approximately one half of a blue-book page. (2) It should be understood that rejection of a Big Lie does not imply acceptance of its contrary. I recognize that the contraries are just as untrue and just as pernicious as the lies I have listed; thus, I have footnoted those contraries throughout the text. (3) Contrary Big Lie: Deaf people are limited to simple menial, manual and clerical tasks. (4) Contrary Big Lie: Being deaf is devastating; a deaf person cannot have a "normal" life. (5) Contary Big Lie: It is morally wrong to sign without speaking or to speak without signing, ever, even in the privacy of one's own home, car, etc. (6) Contrary Big Lie: Nothing can be done; Gallaudet should either send all our students home and close up shop or accept that we cannot really do what we say we do. (7) Contrary Big Lie: Spokespersons for Gallaudet should stress the things our students cannot do. (8) Contrary Big Lie: Nothing can be done; Gallaudet should either send all our students home and close up shop or accept that we cannot really do what we say we do. (9) Contrary Big Lie: The quality of life of a deaf person who socializes almost exclusively with other deaf persons, who is educated in schools especially for deaf persons, and whose career is in the field of deafness will be manifestly *inferior* to the quality of life of a deaf person who achieves success independent of institutions for the deaf and of the society of other deaf people. (10) Contrary Big Lie: All wisdom lies in the faculty, which is manifestly more able to run the university than is the administration. (11) Contrary Big Lie: If the lazy, shiftless bums in the faculty would get off their butts and do their jobs, then we administrators wouldn't have to bail so hard to keep this place afloat. (12) I.e., that prelingual deafness is not just a lifestyle choice; that it is a real disability, one which can be partially or wholly overcome but one which has a profound impact on all those it strikes, and that, in general, the less one can hear and the earlier the age of onset, the more profound the effects of the disability are likely to be. (13) "Know thyself." Socrates. (14) "The unexamined life is not worth living." Socrates. "It's also a damned sight more difficult than it needs to be." Stelle.

ASL: SHATTERING THE MYTH

From: Truman Stelle
To: Whom It May Concern
Subject: Addendum to Vision Statement

I just wanted to clarify my intention on a couple of the points I made in my now-notorious vision statement. I think I was a bit abrupt and failed to communicate clearly:

1. With respect to Big Lies #1 and #2, I can interpret the statement "deaf people can do anything but hear," in three very different ways: (a) It points toward an ideal, a goal with which I fully agree. (b) It is a statement of literal fact; there are deaf persons, probably prelingually deaf persons, in virtually every job you can name. (c) It is a claim that deafness is just what it seems to be at first glance -- an inability to hear, more than an annoyance but less than a major handicap -- and that it has no other significant implications. This I am sure is how the general public interprets this statement.

This third interpretation sets up unrealistic expectations. Supported primarily by tax money, Gallaudet has a responsibility not only to our students but to our funders, Congress and the taxpayers, who have a right to know what they're buying with their $70-80 million *[per year]*. When we tell them that deaf people are just like everyone else except that they have a hearing loss, (I know that some object to the use of the term "hearing loss;" I don't know of a term that isn't objected to by someone, often for reasonable reasons.) we know that they will infer from that statement that *most* of our graduates have knowledge and skills comparable with those of the graduates of most other colleges and universities. Anyone who has been on this campus for more than a week or two and who is not comatose is aware that such an inference simply is not true. And most employers find out that it is not true the first time they hire one of ours for a professional position that requires writing.

Gallaudet has, in the past 20+ years, become very popular with the general public. Part of this is due to our public relations efforts. But advertising serves mainly to get the potential consumer to try the product once; after that, the hype fades into relative insignificance while the experience of actually trying the product becomes paramount. I suspect that many private sector employers who hire our students once, expecting professional-level literacy skills, do not come back to us for a second helping because they feel they've been "had." (And very likely they tell their pals about their experiences.) Creating false expectations has the ultimate effect of creating distrust, and once you've lost your public's trust you've lost the whole ballgame; without credibility nothing else matters. And let's not kid ourselves; this means that more and more of our graduates will be working for government, and eventually the word will get to the people who have to vote on our appropriations. Unless they're so crazy about what we symbolize that they really don't care what we do, the question is not whether our dysfunctional secret will get out, but when.

2. With respect to Big Lie #7, I simply wish that when he was offered the opportunity to write that book review for the *[Washington] Post*, instead of trying to score a cheap point for Gallaudet and its narrow interests, *[Gallaudet President]* I.K.J. had used that forum, that "bully pulpit," to educate the public a bit, explaining the effects of prelingual deafness on language development and saying what a marvelous achievement this man had made, a prelingually profoundly deaf man who is a book reviewer for a respected large-city newspaper.

[Reprinted with permission from Truman Stelle]

76

CHAPTER FOUR

LANGUAGE AND LITERACY
by Otto J. Menzel

[Dr. Menzel is a retired clinical audiologist and a former teacher who became deaf 22 years ago. Currently the editor of "Life After Deafness," he has written numerous deafness-related essays including over 60 articles for professional journals. He is also the co-author of "Feud for Thought," a satire about the petty division among the many factions of deaf people]

TO: BOARD OF DIRECTORS,   October 7, 1996
NATIONAL COUNCIL OF ACCREDITATION OF
TEACHER EDUCATION (NCATE)
2010 Massachusetts Avenue NW
Washington, D.C. 20036

This letter is in reference to the impending review of the accreditation status of the Gallaudet University School of Education and Human Services. The undersigned is (a) an audiologist of several decades' standing, (b) a deaf man, (c) editor of a magazine for deafened people, (d) a former teacher, (e) a tax payer, and (f) an amicus curiae. In all those capacities I firmly oppose accreditation of the Gallaudet program.

The obvious purpose of any school of education is to prepare students to become qualified teachers. Presumably, graduates of the Gallaudet program will seek employment as teachers of the deaf.

ENGLISH LITERACY

The most formidable challenge to confront any teacher of the deaf is to make the pupils literate in English. This has always been so, but the importance of it has grown substantially in recent years because of the demands of the "information age" generally and also because of the technological advances that have affected the lives of deaf people specifically. Text telephones and relay services, closed captioned television, "on-line" computer services, facsimile machines -- all these have greatly enhanced life for deaf people and brought them closer to mainstream society, *provided they have reasonable competency in English and can read and write!*

The typical graduate of a typical residential school for the deaf in America has reading skills no better than third or fourth grade level. Three out of four cannot read a newspaper. According to Winfield McChord, the average deaf pupil in a residential school spends no more than 7% of his time in any class, probably only 1% in English class! Unlike hearing children, he Is NOT exposed to English outside of class, such as via family, radio, television, or playmates; neither is he likely to do any reading for pleasure, since he has not learned to read. How is he to acquire adequate English language skills that way? David Bartlett, in 1852, said, "To educate the deaf is to teach them language." Alexander Graham Bell emphasized, "It is reading, reading, reading that will give our pupils mastery of the English language." When Helen Keller's mother asked Anne Sullivan what she would try to teach Helen first, Ms. Sullivan replied, "First, last and in between, language.

Language is to the mind more than light is to the eye." Yes, and the language Anne Sullivan taught Helen Keller was English!

Yet another notable educator of the deaf, E. L. Scouten, who taught at Gallaudet for a number of years, pointed out, "For too long our educational perspective has been dominated by a gestural surrogate to the neglect of orthographic language, in our case English, our language of business, science, and industry." He went on to say that "The hearing world is not to be down-played. It is an ever-present reality with which our prelingually deaf children and youth must learn to come to grips. They cannot successfully come to grips with this hearing world if they cannot at least read and write adequately their own national language."

HOW ENGLISH IS LEARNED

English, like any language, is best learned by immersion, by being surrounded by it continuously, by being forced to use it exclusively. The undersigned learned English as a third language fast and well by being placed in an ordinary public school setting where English was the sole language used, for all purposes. There was no special "bilingual" instruction, no recourse to previously learned languages. One does not learn to swim on dry land, nor does one learn English through American Sign Language. One learns English through English itself.

That is nothing new, yet it is a concept that seems to have been forgotten at Gallaudet!

A number of respected deaf educators have emphasized the need for English to be used pervasively. "Every teacher, no matter what subject, should also be a teacher of English to some extent." (R. F. Panara) "The responsibility for language usage-practice must be shared by the teachers of *all* disciplines, and houseparents as well," (Scouten) "Teachers must understand that the language aspect of curriculum is an integral part of every discipline. For deaf children and youth there are no non-language subjects." (Scouten) "Writing can only be taught by the united efforts of the entire teaching staff." (Barzun, quoted by Panara).

SIGN LANGUAGE VIS-A-VIS ENGLISH

Throughout most of the history of American deaf education, sign language has been used. Until comparatively recently, the several variants of it were largely based on English-word-order, such as "Signed Exact English," "English Sign Language," "English Signs," and several other variants. These sundry sign languages were useful in teaching English, because of grammatical similarity, supplemented at times by fingerspelling. American Sign Language (ASL) was "discovered" by William Stokoe less than twenty years ago when he ascertained that the informal gestural language used mainly by deaf children among themselves *[in particular, at residential schools for the deaf]* had its own grammar separate and distinct from English grammar. Similar assertions can be made about various "pidgin" languages or others that constitute simplified ways of communicating. Despite statements as to the complexity, flexibility and expressiveness of ASL, from its enthusiasts, the language is severely limited compared to English, quite incapable of expressing many nuances available to a person thoroughly conversant (pun unintended, yet apt) with English. Perhaps even more important is the fact ASL has no written form. There are no textbooks in ASL. no newspapers, no instruction manuals, no job application forms et cetera.

In the words of yet another prominent deaf educator, L. G. Stewart, "ASL, as linguistically defined, has nowhere near the power of English for receptive OR expressive purposes. ASL has its own merits, some of them outshining spoken language, but anywhere near as powerful as English for education, commerce, and all around communication purposes it most certainly is not."

Sign language is unquestionably an important tool for use with -- and by -- prelingually deaf children. Its use as a "first" language to serve as a stepping stone to English, as well as a means of early "bonding" with parents and siblings, has clear value. Its use, however, should never prevent let alone preclude the early introduction to English. Insofar as the acquisition of English as early as possible is a prime objective, any sign language used in those early stages should be one of the several systems based on English, and NOT ASL, possibly excepting the case of a child whose parents know only ASL.

THE GALLAUDET *FAILURE*

The celebrated "Deaf President Now" revolt at Gallaudet in 1988 has led to unexpected consequences. Quite aside from the more recently established facts about that incident, which show that the "revolt" was actually instigated by persons who were not students, and that there was considerable distortion of the events by the media, those events gave rise to some new, chauvinistic attitudes among both students and faculty. Somehow, the events of 1988 gave rise to "deaf pride" and "deaf culture," both of which are political creations, not anthropological realities. (Stewart) They also gave rise to a fanatical movement, supported by both students and faculty and tolerated by a weak administration, which strives to further segregate the deaf from the mainstream of American society. Among the incomprehensible but strong advocacies of these radicals is the strange insistence on rejecting the use of English, the teaching of English, and even tolerance of English usage by deaf persons capable of using it. There in a "NO VOICE" faction that seeks to prevent any teacher from using spoken English in class and to stop spoken English usage in general, instead confining all communication, including classroom instruction, to ASL. Never mind that there are no textbooks in ASL and that all textbooks are useless to those whose sole language is ASL.

Another prominent faction is the "Bi-Bi" movement. The acronym stands for "Bilingual-Bicultural." This term is misleading, however. The "Bi-Bi" approach emphasizes teaching ASL (no English-based sign language, but strictly ASL) to the deaf child, intensively and extensively, until everyone is sure ASL has become his "first and native" language and he is thoroughly proficient in it. Then and only then, English is introduced as a "second language," (by which is meant a secondary language) taught in the classroom using ASL as the language of instruction! Obviously this, again, is done without textbooks, since ASL has no written form and the child that has not yet learned English can't read a textbook.

T. Balkany et al, citing the National Association of the Deaf Position Paper on ASL (1994), describes it thus: "A fable of inverted 'Wonderland' logic . . . concludes that failure among people fluent in ASL to read English is the result of too little training in ASL. Solution -- teach less English and more ASL."

ASL: SHATTERING THE MYTH

Such twisted logic, alas, has become the credo of a number of faculty members at Gallaudet -- by no means all -- who are teaching via ASL exclusively, using no speech (not even mouthing), and preaching that ASL is sufficient for all communication needs of the deaf, and that "Bi-Bi" is the way to teach in the primary and secondary schools for the deaf. According to Stewart, the credo of the "Bi-Bi" advocates includes this statement: "Deaf teachers do not need to pass a national test of English proficiency because such tests are discriminatory in view of the fact that the natural language of the deaf is ASL."

Predictably, Gallaudet students and graduates -- the very ones who plan to become teachers of the deaf -- are so abysmally lacking in minimal English language skills that most of them are unemployable in any setting other than residential schools for the deaf, and there only because such schools are notoriously unconcerned about such things. According to one Gallaudet faculty member, Gallaudet has received a number of letters from government agencies and private businesses indicating they can no longer hire Gallaudet graduates because they simply cannot read and write (Parsons). According to *[Lew]* Golan, a sheltered academically undemanding atmosphere at Gallaudet is leaving students unprepared for jobs in the mainstream society.

Further observations by Stewart: "How on earth do we expect proper English to be learned by deaf students if there is no standard of English usage among teachers, both deaf and hearing, for both modeling and instructional purposes?" "One thing we can be sure of: Poor English usage on the part of the teacher, deaf or hearing, will adversely affect English competency development in deaf children."

PROFICIENCY IN ASL IS NOT AN ALTERNATIVE TO LITERACY

Obviously any "University" whose graduates are only borderline literate is not deserving of the name, to begin with, but to "market" such graduates as qualified teachers is preposterous. Accreditation of such a program by a responsible accrediting agency is unthinkable.

It is not surprising that, according to Deaf Life magazine, 70% of graduates of residential deaf schools are on the Social Security Disability rolls, and receive Supplemental Security Income (SSI) to boot. Until those schools employ and support teachers who can and will teach deaf children English as well as other subjects, teachers who obviously have a good command of English themselves, and until they employ houseparents with similar attitudes and commensurate qualifications, and until the deaf children are given an education that enables them to obtain and hold jobs in some self-supporting line of work, the worst fears of the radical proponents of "deaf culture" will be realized *precisely because of their own misguided efforts to forestall the demise of "deaf culture."* And until the Gallaudet University School of Education and Human Services divests itself of radicals on its faculty and adopts a rational plan for training teachers and for turning out literate graduates, it will not merit accreditation.

[Reprinted with permission from Otto Menzel]

84

CHAPTER FIVE

CRITICAL THINKING ABOUT ASL
by Patrick W. Seamans

[Patrick Seamans was born profoundly deaf, and his first language is French. He has a masters degree in Teaching English as a Second Language, and he was a National Leadership Fellow for TESOL International. He is currently completing his PhD in International and Intercultural Education.]

A BRIEF HISTORY OF ASL

Around 1760, a school for the deaf was established by the Abbe de l'Epee in France, who later in 1784 published the influential landmark guide "The True Way to Educate the Deaf." After l'Epee's death in 1789, Roch-Ambroise Sicard took over operation of the school, and published the widely distributed fingerspelled alphabet for the deaf, and the first textbook for educating the deaf in sign language.

During a trip to London in 1815, Sicard presented his best deaf pupil, Laurent Clerc, to members of Parliament and large crowds of spectators, which included Thomas Hopkins Gallaudet, an American visiting Europe seeking to acquire the art of instructing the deaf. Gallaudet took up Sicard's invitation to learn the French method and later returned to the U.S. with Laurent Clerc and established the American School for the Deaf in Hartford, Connecticut, in 1817. The institutions for the deaf set up by Gallaudet and Clerc were established with a goal students to sign in proper English-word-order and away from the "street signs" many used at the time. "Street signs" pretty much describes what ASL is today. During a speech at the opening of Gallaudet College in 1864, Clerc said there was now widespread education of the deaf available and there was no reason anymore to have illiterate deaf people. He noted that English-illiterate deaf persons were "barbarians."

It wasn't until 1863 when the "oralism" approach appeared. It focused on making the deaf person "look like a hearing person," and hearing parents of deaf children were very susceptible to those arguments. The "manualists" did not notice this new development until Edward Miner Gallaudet, the son of Thomas Hopkins Gallaudet, called a conference of school principals of manualist schools, which resulted in a decision to combine oralism into their curricula, creating the "oral-manual" method. The consensus was not to abandon signs in favor of a pure oral method, but to utilize both elements judiciously.

Around 1868, Alexander Graham Bell, a supporter of the pure oralism method, and Edward Miner Gallaudet constantly disagreed which approach was best for the deaf students. Battle lines were drawn for a conflict that still rages today. This controversy resulted in the 1880 Milan Conference in Italy which selected the oral method for the schools for the deaf, both in the United States and Europe. This action totally destroyed the use of any form of manualism *[sign language]* for educating the deaf in France. A minority of schools in the United States, including Gallaudet University, retained the oral-manual method. While the United States was able to retain the "old" system of French-American methodical signs, the French lost their system almost completely.

ASL: SHATTERING THE MYTH

In the "dark ages" that followed, it became obvious that the oralism approach would never be totally successful with all prelingually deaf children. One problem was most prelingually profound deaf children simply could not see all the sounds being made. This situation has been corrected by Cued Speech training which makes all language sounds 100% visible. After years of oralism failures, English-based manual communication once again rose to prominence. However, in recent decades, deaf education has moved from the English-word-order system of signing back to the old "street signs" of ASL, which were used by illiterate and uneducated deaf individuals prior to the establishment, under the guidance of Laurent Clerc, of formalized deaf education in the U.S.

CLEAR THINKING ABOUT LANGUAGES

"Is American Sign Language (ASL) a separate language or not?" The disagreement over this issue has caused a split within both the deaf community and the community of hearing people who work with them. The clash of opinions is astounding, and is very important, since, obviously, you cannot have a "bilingual/bicultural" program unless you have two separate, distinct languages.

On one hand, we have a group of professional linguists and educators along with members of the deaf community, who strongly assert that ASL cannot be a "separate language" because, among other things:

(a) There is no true path to language development for all deaf children, since there are variations in hearing ability, intelligence, background, etc.
(b) No one can agree on the exact form of ASL that fits criteria of a separate language since all residential schools teach different signs.
(c) There are no inflections in manual language; reading ability is slower for multiple meanings; no passive forms, no reliable time indicators, no syntax without additional body language and mime, and no means to

87

ASL: SHATTERING THE MYTH

express clearly enough differences in function of subject, direct object and indirect object.

(d) Most members of the "core" deaf community, including deaf children of deaf parents, do not believe that ASL is a separate language, and they do not believe there is such a thing as "Deaf Culture." These people, including most teachers of the deaf, prefer the "middle ground" of the Pidgin Sign Language *[A form of ASL signs in English-word-order]* in order to have effective access to both the deaf and hearing "worlds."

(e) If ASL is supposedly the "natural language of the deaf," then why do only 3% of deaf people (those whose parents are deaf) speak the language exclusively, and why do they prefer the Pidgin form of English?

(f) Why do most deaf people misunderstand a large portion of what they communicate to each other in manual form? Studies show a 30-40% rate of misunderstanding among those who use ASL exclusively in peer-to-peer communication.

(g) Research shows that sign language is an obstacle to abstract thinking in a verbal (spoken and written) language, such as English. Higher education and advanced degrees absolutely require a higher understanding of concepts over observed elements.

(h) The average deaf child who uses ASL primarily, after 11 years of formal schooling, still reads and writes English at only a 3rd or 4th grade level of ability.

If all of the analyses above are correct, then it is apparent that ASL, the purely visual-manual form, is not a separate language. Or, if it is a separate language, it results in misunderstandings and misinformation so often that no one would want to use it as a primary language, anyway. Larry Stewart, a deaf professor at Gallaudet University stated *[see Chapter 1]* that "Bilingual/Bicultural" education is the spread of "intellectual claptrap" in the deaf community, that "the language of the deaf, the culture of the deaf, and the success of deaf education" are pure speculations; and that "this type of hurtful foolishness is being used to brainwash young deaf and hard-of-hearing high school and college students to conform to expectations that they will reject their English backgrounds, oral and signed, and in the process criticize their parents and former hearing teachers for not having used ASL with them."

On the other hand, there is a relatively strong, vocal, minority within the deaf community, a few linguists and other professionals who just as strongly assert that *ASL is* a separate distinct language, resulting in "Deaf Culture," and that there should be both bilingual and bicultural educational programs *[the Bi-Bi approach]*. These people state that ASL is a "language," because of a new application of the word "language" to a nonverbal communication. (The word "language" was formerly used only for verbal languages). They say that you cannot use the linguistic criteria of spoken (verbal) languages to analyze a purely visual-spatial-gestural language. They are correct, which is why there is no such thing as "ASL Linguistics" or "ASL Literacy." ASL is, as they state, properly studied in the field of Nonverbal Communication, not in the field of Linguistics, which studies verbal languages. And "literacy" only applies to the reading and writing of verbal languages in printed form. However, most of the ASL/Deaf culture activists misunderstand this distinction, and assert that, because ASL is now called a "language," it should be the language of instruction for the deaf in schools. This is completely untrue, since the language of instruction for all students in the U.S. is English.

Most of the deaf educators and the general deaf community see this "activist" viewpoint as possibly interesting, but mostly "extremist," since it advocates segregated education, lifestyle and attitudes, and discrimination against the hearing world, and results in an inability to independently communicate in English.

Approximately 3% of profoundly deaf persons, those with deaf parents, speak the true ASL in purely visual form.

Most deaf parents also realize that their children must be educated in the spoken, written language of their country, and they tend to send their deaf children to "mainstream" programs in regular schools.

There is also a major push for ASL in the schools within a Bi-Bi curriculum. These Deaf Culture/Deaf Language advocates assert that ASL is a natural sign language, which must be taught in residential schools operated by deaf teachers and administrators, or else their "Culture" will be lost. There has also been a fear, primarily created by deaf teachers and administrators in the residential schools (who want to save their own jobs) that the focus on "mainstreaming" would lead to the destruction of the deaf community.

This movement towards "Bilingual/Bicultural" education programs and the consideration of ASL as a "separate" language, is a new, growing attempt by a *very few* ASL supporters in the deaf community to assert their pride, independence and self-esteem. They seem to be basing their identities on ideology *[and emotions]* instead of science, and on the fact that they are primarily "Deaf," instead of on the fact that they are primarily normal human beings with hearing problems. *[These ASL supporters would benefit from reading Carl Sagan's excellent book "The Demon-Haunted World," a critique of uncritical thinking. This is a problem that is plaguing the deaf community and many professionals who have rushed to embrace ASL without applying skepticism.]* In this respect, the effort towards the desired communication function of "sign language without voice" from this movement is a corpus planning attempt, with the hopes that the structure of both schools and society will change as a result. "Corpus planning" is an attempt by a group of people to change the language used for educating students, thus changing their perspectives on life and cultural orientation -- One example: in Africa where French language and national curriculum replaced the national African languages. In the deaf community, although more than 90% of deaf children are born of hearing parents or became deaf later in life, the ASL supporters are trying to replace their "natural" language -- English -- with ASL. Many feel this is just an attempt to "steal" children from their homes and families to get more "numbers" to help the ASL supporters justify the cost to society to support all ASL-related services and programs. Another example of "corpus planning" is how hearing parents are being misled by ASL supporters by exposure to many "profiles" of "success stories" in prominent deaf-related periodicals. In many cases they received English-based education earlier in life and were already literate. The icing on the cake would be how these newly-created ASL users will later discriminate against and insult their own parents and teachers for teaching them to communicate independently in English, instead of having taught them in ASL, which results in functional illiteracy and a need to depend on interpreters for the rest of their lives.

The current organized efforts to have ASL recognized as a *second* language is gaining momentum among educators and politicians. However, the extremist movement to make ASL a *first* language of the deaf has been largely rejected. Interestingly, now that ASL is included as a "foreign language" in many school systems, more hearing people are learning ASL than deaf people; thus it may no longer be a "natural language for people who cannot hear."

In 1998, reports have come from the National Research Council, and other professional agencies, about the problems in teaching children to read and write English. These reports are based on scientific research, and they reject assertions based totally on ideology or "feelings." The reports clearly indicate that training in phonemics (the sounds of the English language) is required as a prerequisite to learning to decode printed materials, and to read and write fluently in English. The Cued Speech method is the only scientifically-proven way to provide 100% of the sounds of the English language visually to any deaf person.

Both hearing and deaf individuals need to learn both verbal and nonverbal communication, for complete and independent lives. Research shows that approximately 60% of communication is "nonverbal." But, as Laurent Clerc noted, deaf individuals must train themselves to use verbal language to understand the "other 40%" of communication they miss without proper instruction in English.

For reading and understanding of the sounds of English represented by the printed characters, it is necessary to use either oral methods or Cued Speech. Once these sounds are learned fully, they are permanently in the mind. Deaf individuals can choose to also learn ASL, for social and emotional communication, but, according to research, the art of thoroughly seeing nonverbal communication (pure ASL) is extremely difficult.

In the U.S., fluency in reading and writing English is an absolute necessity for all, and so is the ability for deaf people to listen and communicate in clear English through the use of cueing or signing English Transliterators. Once the ability to use English has been mastered, anyone may personally choose to learn any other foreign language and culture, including ASL and Deaf Culture, which is widely available in special ASL foreign (non-English) language courses, and in activities and materials provided by deaf organizations, clubs and groups.

[Submitted by Patrick Seamans]

CHAPTER SIX

Review of: MASK OF BENEVOLENCE, A book review by Donald F. Moores

[Dr. Moores is a Professor of Education at Gallaudet and is editor of the "American Annals of the Deaf." Dr. Moores' excellent critical analysis of Harlan Lane's book deserves widespread exposure simply because Lane wrote many of the covenants of deaf culture (and ASL-as-a-language) which were all too readily adopted by many without the necessary critical thinking and scrutiny normally applied to such things.]

The Mask of Benevolence: Disabling the Deaf Community
Author: Harlan Lane. (New York: Alfred A. Knopf, 1992)

It was with a sense of anticipation that I began this latest book by Harlan Lane. I had read The Wild Boy of Aveyron and The Wild Boy of Burundi in addition to many of his publications on deafness and had been impressed by his articulateness and commitment. I found him to be concerned and sensitive.

In this book Lane identifies several important issues of concern to the field of deaf education including, but not limited to, moral and practical questions related to invasive surgical techniques such as cochlear implants with young deaf children, continued lack of acceptance in some quarters of American Sign Language (ASL), underrepresentation of deaf professionals in positions of authority, low academic achievement in deaf children of normal intellectual potential, and invalid and unreliable assessment of the cognitive, social-emotional, and academic status of deaf children and adults. He is to be applauded for addressing such a range of problems. Unfortunately, however, his treatment of the issues is so superficial and unidimensional as to distort reality. It was with a sense of profound disappointment, then, that I had to conclude that Lane's latest effort falls far beneath his usual standards.

Lane had the opportunity to make a major contribution with this book, but he lost it. The field of education of the deaf *does* have a long tradition of discrimination against and limited opportunity for deaf people. He could have made the case effectively. Discrimination has existed in the United States since the first school for the deaf was established in the early 19th century and existed in France for generations before that. However, Lane forfeits credibility by sensationalizing the situation and, even more grievous, by betraying his ideals through arrogant, paternalistic, and condescending behavior toward deaf people in general and deaf Africans in particular. His actions, as described in the book, betray a chilling mask of benevolence.

Lane takes complex issues, such as assessment of cognitive and social emotional adjustment of deaf people, educational placement, relationships between ASL and English, and the efficacy or danger of cochlear implants with young children, and in each case reduces the issue into superficial either/or, good/bad dichotomies. He does the same with individuals and even periods of time. For example, according to Lane, the period around the middle of the 19th century was almost a golden age for deaf Americans, and the present time is bad. Such generalizations are simply false. There *were* many positive aspects of life for deaf Americans in the 19th century, but there were also many terrible problems. There *are* many problems of discrimination and lack of access for present-day deaf Americans, but there are also many positive aspects. By refusing to acknowledge this, Lane calls into question his sweeping, often undocumented, claims.

The basic premise of this book is that deaf communities ". . . have suffered repression, in *all of its forms and consequences* [italics added], in common with other cultures that were literally subjugated by imperial powers" (p. 40). According to Lane, the oppression of deaf people is caused by an "audist" establishment dedicated to perpetuating its "antideaf philosophy" and excluding deaf people from its ranks. Audism is "the paternalistic hearing-centered endeavor that professes to serve deaf people." In truth, however, according to Lane, "Audism is the hearing way of dominating, restructuring, and exercising authority over the deaf community" (p. 43). The typical audist is responding to a complex of inferiority; he is compensating. Audists seek to put deaf people in a dependency role and may be drawn to the field by a "dreamlike vision of innocence." Flight from the hearing world may be a major reason why hearing people who may be out of tune with their own society choose to work in the deaf world (p. 76).

By equating the very real problems faced by deaf people with the suffering of colonized people, Lane trivializes the latter and distorts the former. Imperial France, Japan, England, China, America, Russia, and other countries often ruled by brutal, bloody repression and terror while deliberately draining colonies of vital resources. Deaf and hearing parents love and cherish their deaf children in the same way that deaf and hearing parents love and cherish their hearing children and try to provide for them as well as possible.

On the federal level, Lane's charge of imperialist oppression simply does not hold water. An imperial power institutionalizes deliberately oppressive measures against the colonized. There is no evidence of this in the congressional legislation passed in the last generation: quite the opposite is true. Just a few examples should suffice.

Congress passed the Education of the Deaf Act (EDA) of 1986 (PL 99-371) as a means of improving educational opportunities for deaf Americans. Among the outcomes of the 1986 EDA was the establishment of the Commission on Education of the Deaf, [CED] chaired by a deaf professional. Dr. Frank G. Bowe. The commission identified several areas of weakness and need and presented to the president of the United States and Congress a report (Commission on Education of the Deaf, 1988) containing 52 recommendations. Bowe (1991) reported that within three years, half of the recommendations had been acted on. At present, Bowe has concluded that major progress has been made on most recommendations. The EDA Amendments of 1992 (PL 102-42) implemented many of the recommendations. The Rehabilitation Act Amendments of 1992 (102-569) took further action in support of deaf people. On October 30, 1992, the U.S. Department of Education issued a "Notice of Policy Guidance" clarifying its views on CED recommendations concerning appropriate education, least restrictive environment, student evaluation, and curriculum, among other issues.

Bowe concluded that the changes implemented represent significant steps forward on behalf of deaf children, youth, and adults. The federal response certainly does not reflect an imperialist or "antideaf" philosophy, as Lane claims. Other examples of federal support include the Television Decoder Act (PL 101-431), which mandates that most new TV sets be caption capable by 1993, and Title IV of the Americans With Disabilities Act, which authorizes TDD-voice telephone relays. One may disagree with specifics of any of the legislation, but the federal intent is obviously supportive, not repressive.

One might wonder how Lane came to be the only member of the oppressor hearing class to recognize and oppose repression. He explains it in his book quite simply. In any oppressing class there are a few who do not accept their reality as oppressors. Clearly, Lane sees himself as one of the few. Of these few, one, a renegade, may struggle for more equal distribution of power. Clearly, again, Lane is the one renegade from the oppressor class who is struggling for a more equal distribution of power. Lane explains his role as follows, "What then can a hearing person of goodwill do? Karl Marx said that the role of the bourgeois intelligentsia was to hasten the revolution" (p. 87). Following a Marxist directive, Lane, as a hearing person of goodwill, self-consciously portrays himself as a hearing bourgeois intellectual hastening a revolution.

Lane claims the audist establishment, and its organizations, ". . . disseminates the information it produces through the professional journals that it publishes, such as the *American Annals of the Deaf,* published by the Convention of American Instructors of the Deaf and the Conference of Educational Administrators of [*sic*] the Deaf." (p. 70). He states:

> There is exceedingly little of the deaf point of view to be found in the *Annals* or any other audist journal or in conference proceedings. This is not the result, generally, of conscious

malevolent attempts to suppress information. Rather, views that have a deaf "center" seem to audists wildly at odds with prevailing views, unworthy of dissemination, and the credentials of the people who present these views or the methods they employ may seem unconventional: For example, the rejected study may have surveyed deaf people themselves rather than professionals who work with deaf people, or ethnographic methods may have been used rather than those arising from educational psychology.

As editor of the Annals, I know our deaf and hearing reviewers cannot judge the credentials of authors, simply because names of authors are not provided. I also know that these two "audist" organizations -- the Convention of American Instructors of the Deaf (CAID) and the Conference of Educational Administrators Serving the Deaf (CEASD), with their "guiding antideaf philosophy, and with the exclusion of deaf people from its ranks" -- each has a deaf professional as president in 1993. The Annals editor serves at the pleasure of a joint CAID/CEASD committee that selects the editor and establishes policy. In 1992, four of the seven committee members were deaf. In 1993, three of seven are deaf. Lane's claims of an oppressive audist establishment are woefully out of touch with current realities.

Lane frequently compares the present situation unfavorably with conditions in the early to middle 19th century when, he claims, there was equality between deaf and hearing professionals, there was no medical or pathological model of deafness, and academic achievement was much higher. This situation changed, according to Lane (p. 25), when hearing people seized control of education of the deaf. Lane is correct in pointing up the difficulties faced by deaf people today, but he wants to return to the halcyon days of a mythical past that never was.

ASL: SHATTERING THE MYTH

On balance, life for deaf Americans in the middle of the 19th century was much worse than it is today. Fewer than half of all deaf children in 19th century America ever set foot in a school for the deaf, and whole groups were excluded, most glaringly deaf African-Americans. The first school for "Negro" or "Colored" deaf children was not established until after the Civil War. Deaf children typically did not start school until age 10 or older and four or five years of instruction was the norm. As evidence for the influence of deaf teachers, Lane states that before the Conference of Milan in 1880 "American deaf teachers had founded 24 schools for deaf children" (p. 116). As in so many cases in the book, Lane cites no source for this statement, which is incorrect. Jack Gannon's *Deaf Heritage* (1981, p. 18) lists nine residential and day schools for the deaf established by deaf teachers before the Milan Conference. In fact more were established *after* Milan than before, a fact that refutes Lane's basic assumptions.

The sad reality that Lane ignores is that the education of the deaf for most of the past century was under the control of paternalistic, rigid, authoritarian hearing men who regarded deaf people, as well as women, African Americans, Jews, Catholics, and many others as inferior. If these men did not have a medical-pathological model of deafness, they did have a missionary model. In response to a paper by Weed (1859) on the missionary element in deaf education, the Reverend W. W. Turner, principal of the American School for the Deaf, stated:

> It is greatly to be desired that teachers of the Deaf and Dumb should keep steadily before them this great object, which was so prominently before the minds of those who introduced the art of teaching mutes into this country -- the spiritual elevation of those admitted to their care. The deaf and dumb when they come into our institutions are heathen. (p. 30)

99

There are ample examples of oppression of deaf people in the 19th century. At the third meeting of CAID in 1853, it was decided, over the opposition of Laurent Clerc, that the procedure on any question would be for a voice vote by hearing participants, to be followed with a show of hands by the deaf participants. It was not until the seventh CAID meeting in 1870 that the question of allowing deaf and female participants to serve on committees was even raised. The insensitivity of hearing educators is best illustrated by the response of Harvey Peet, as reported in the 1853 CAID proceedings, to the request for voting by a show of hands.

> Dr. Peet said he would not exactly oppose this motion, hut he thought practical application would be found inconvenient. To him it would he altogether the most satisfactory that the question be taken by ayes and noes, the Deaf Mutes themselves voting by the uplifted hand. The vote could in no case be simultaneous because the Deaf Mutes must necessarily have the matter explained.

> This he thought, would be annoying and calculated to retard business . . . He proposed that the vote of the Deaf Mutes be taken after the votes by ayes and noes.

Peet's proposal was accepted. Lest one think that Peet represented a minority view, it should be pointed out that Lane (1992) identified Peet as superintendent of the New York Institution, first president of CAID, "the dean of American educators of the deaf," and a man who "had long been the intellectual leader of his profession" (p. 265).

The most stark example of the repression under which deaf teachers had to labor in Lane's supposedly golden age of the 19th century is provided by the vicious reaction by hearing administrators to the request of John Carlin, a deaf artist; poet, and community leader, that schools for the deaf follow a

principle of equal pay for equal work and raise the salaries of deaf teachers to the same level as those of hearing teachers. After pursuing the topic for several years, Carlin submitted his request by letter to the fifth meeting of CAID, in 1858. Following are some of the comments published in the meeting proceedings in 1859.

> Mute teachers are not capable of doing that for which we need liberally educated men (p. 70).
>
> *Samuel Porter,*
> *American School*

> He (the deaf teacher) is not in full communion with his fellow-beings and never can be. It is the want of this that incapacitates him for the accomplishment of the higher duties of a teacher (p. 71).
>
> *Rev. W. W. Turner.*
> *Principal, American School*

> It is Mr. Carlin, who is not a teacher and never will be -- because he can do a great deal better in his present lucrative and honorable profession . . . although I have a great deal of respect for him (Carlin), and own that *for a deaf and dumb man, I could never understand how he could get such an education* (italics added). (p. 73)
>
> *Rev. B. M. Fay*
> *Principal, Michigan School*

> I believe that a man deprived of one important sense is not as valuable as a man who has use of all. I do not subscribe to the doctrine that a deaf and dumb teacher can become as useful as a speaking teacher.
>
> *Rev. Collins Stone,*
> *Superintendent, Ohio School*

The issue was decided by Harvey Peet, Lane's "dean" of American educators of the deaf and "intellectual leader of his profession." In a devastating response to Carlin's request, Peet stated:

> Beyond a certain point, the deaf mute teacher is not as well qualified to carry on a class as a hearing and speaking man. In the first place, he is not as well educated. There are a great many idioms of the language he does not and can not understand . . . This is precisely the argument brought forward by all the woman's rights conventions in the country that I have ever heard of. They say if a female performs certain duties as well as a man, for instance, those of a clerk, she ought to have the same salary that a man gets. I am disposed to doubt and controvert this idea. (p. 66)

> The deaf and dumb teachers do not perform as much service as a professor. For instance, they have nothing to do with performing religious worship in the chapel . . . And they are not capable of carrying a class to as high a degree of attainment. It would be very unwise indeed to place a class of four or five years standing under a deaf mute teacher. (p. 67)

> They are not qualified to carry forward a class of Deaf Mutes, successfully, for over a period of three to four years. (p. 69)

> If I have anything to do with the controlling management of the Institution. I will never allow a deaf mute to go forward with the same class beyond three years.

Note that these chillingly arrogant and oppressive opinions were expressed by a man described by Lane as the intellectual leader of the profession during a time that Lane paints as almost a golden age in which hearing people thought of deaf people "predominantly in terms of a cultural model" and deaf adults "played a prominent role in education."A time when "there were no special educators; the requisites of a good teacher were a good education and fluency in ASL; nearly half of all teachers were deaf themselves." It is hard to imagine how Lane missed the undeniable prejudice against deaf teachers by hearing administrators in the 19th century. The distinction made by Peet and others between hearing "professors" and deaf "teachers" says it all. Rev. Turner, Rev. Fay, Rev. Stone, Mr. Porter, and Dr. Peet -- leaders of the most prestigious schools for the deaf in America in the middle of the 19th century -- displayed a shocking ignorance of the talents of deaf teachers in particular and of the value of deaf human beings in general. It seems as if Lane filters harsh 19th century reality through his own dreamlike vision of innocence.

Lane's (p. 32) claim is that education of the deaf in this century has drifted badly off course from the ideals of the 19th century. Unfortunately, education of the deaf was not on course in the 19th century. We will never solve the very real problems of today by trying to recreate an illusory past. For example, Lane (p. 42) notes that in 1991 there were only 12 deaf superintendents of schools for deaf children, compared to 96 schools with hearing superintendents. These numbers simply are not accurate. There are not 108 schools for the deaf in the United States, as Lane implies. The 1992 Reference Issue of the *American Annals of the Deaf* lists 60 to 65 such schools, depending upon the definition. As in so many cases, Lane cites no source for his figures, thereby calling into question once again the validity of his statements.

It is undeniable that deaf leaders are underrepresented at administrative levels as many educators, including myself, have noted. Still, it would do no good to return to the past century where Lane claims there were deaf administrators of residential schools. It should be pointed out that not one of the schools represented at the 1858 CAID meeting had a deaf superintendent. In fact CAID did not have a deaf president for its first 125 years, until Robert Davila was elected in 1975 (Jack Gannon, personal communication). Davila also later became the first deaf president of CEASD. As noted earlier, the 1993 presidents of both organizations are deaf. Despite our problems, a return to 19th century oppression would be foolish.

One of the most perplexing aspects of the book is that it contains so many inexplicable inaccuracies and misstatements that are obvious to anyone knowledgeable about education of the deaf. After coming across a number of these, I found myself unable to accept any of Lane's statements of "fact" at face value. Perhaps two examples will illustrate this.

Lane (p. 246) refers to an investigation by T. E. Allen and J. Woodward (1987), which he correctly referenced as American Annals of the Deaf 132, 61-67. Lane states, "These investigators sampled 50,000 deaf students and found that 85 percent of the 609 teachers were hearing females. Only 3 percent were deaf." The outside reader has no reason to doubt that these figures are accurate. However *not one of them was presented in the 1987 Allen and Woodward article.*

First, Allen and Woodward sampled 4,500 students, not 50,000. Second, they reported on 885 teachers out of a base of 1,762. The figure 609 is never mentioned. Third, they did not report the gender of the teachers. There is no way to claim from the data that 85% were hearing females. The statement that only 3% of the teachers were deaf is wrong. Allen and Woodward reported that 100 of 885, or 11.3%, of the teachers were deaf and 44 of 885, 5.0%, were hard of hearing.

I was left wondering why Lane presented his material in such a way. If he wanted to break down teachers of the deaf by hearing status and gender, the material is available elsewhere. Where did the figure of 609 teachers come from? If Lane wanted to show that there are too few deaf teachers, the fact is forcefully demonstrated by the very low figure of only 11.3%. Why invent 3%?

ASL: SHATTERING THE MYTH

The second example of an inaccuracy is Lane's statement that "deaf children in America, starting in the late 1970's, were increasingly placed in public schools" (p. 26). Lane apparently equates the phenomenon with the passage of PL 94-142 in 1975 and implementation in the late 70s. In fact the process started shortly after World War II, and the biggest shift occurred *before* 1975. Residential school enrollment dropped from 62% of all deaf students in 1960 to 38% in 1975. The *growth* in public school enrollment from 1960 to 1975 was greater than the *total* public residential enrollment in 1975 (Moores, 1992). If Lane is not aware of basic long-term trends in education of the deaf, his credibility once again is undermined.

As a writer and editor, I am well aware of the difficulties involved in ensuring that all references and data are accurate. From first draft to rewrite to final publication, dates can get transposed and figures miscopied, and not picked up in the proofing process. It is not my intention to belabor minor mistakes, but the fact of the matter is that Lane presents inaccurate information too frequently for comfort.

In equating educators of the deaf with colonizers, Lane excoriates Belgian colonizers in Burundi for their ignorance about the society and their arrogance in refusing to acknowledge existing realities and accomplishments. In reference to the colonizers, Lane states, "It suited them to see the Natives as children, for this confirmed the Africans' need of Belgian guidance and control" (p. 33). Sadly, Lane is not aware that when he set out to help "establish" national education of the deaf in Burundi he treated Africans, especially deaf Africans, as children in need of Lane's guidance and control. His hubris should be an object lesson for all of us.

ASL: SHATTERING THE MYTH

At a reception at Northeastern University in Massachusetts Lane lamented to an official from Burundi the lack of schools for the deaf and offered to help establish national education for the deaf there. They shook hands on it and Lane states, "In 1986, I traveled to Burundi to lay the groundwork for formal education of the deaf in that country" (p. 143). It is hard to believe that as recently as 1986, Lane would set off on his own to establish education of the deaf in a country without at the very least involving professional deaf educators and without seeking support and guidance from organizations of the deaf. Throughout the book, he shows no appreciation of the work of the World Federation of the Deaf or Black Deaf Advocates, an organization of and for deaf African-Americans.

In 1986 he made a presentation at a National Association of the Deaf meeting, where he stated that they may be forced to raise the level of their protest against the audist establishment (p. 186), but gives no indication that he ever asked for advice or help for Burundi. He apparently never sought the advice or support of deaf leaders with international experience such as Yerker Andersson, Merv Garretson, Jack Gannon, or most inexplicably, Andrew Foster, the father of deaf education in black Africa, a deaf African-American and Gallaudet graduate who pioneered the establishment of schools and classes for deaf children throughout the continent, including Burundi. It probably would have been beneficial for Lane if he had studied under Dr. Foster (now deceased) before beginning his work in Burundi. Lane's exclusion of deaf organizations and individuals is especially shocking from someone who advocates equality and empowerment.

En route to Kenya, Lane met a psychologist from Burundi who was also the mother of a deaf child. They joined forces and flew to Burundi, where they visited a Protestant mission that had classes for the deaf. The classes used ASL and French and were established by teachers who had studied in Nigeria under Foster. Lane sought out the rector of the national university and asked him to recommend a graduate who could go to Northeastern University to learn methods of educating deaf children. This person would then return to Burundi and provide courses needed by teachers of the deaf. Lane does not report whether he mentioned to the rector that Northeastern did not have a program to train teachers of the deaf. Lane met with government officials, who approved his plan, and then interviewed and accepted a 27-year-old hearing man who had graduated from the Faculty of Psychology at the national university. The man Lane chose went to Northeastern for two years and then returned to Burundi to open the first "official" school for deaf children in the country. Lane is proud that "hearing people do not yet have a stranglehold on deaf education in Burundi" (p. 153). Of course, he is wrong. A hearing person does have a strangle hold, and the hand around the windpipe belongs to Harlan Lane.

After returning to the United States, Lane decided to write the mother of a 10-year-old deaf child he had observed in a school for the deaf in Burundi for permission to bring the girl to the United States for several years so she could join the American deaf community, continue her education, and eventually become the first deaf teacher of deaf people in Burundi. The parents of the child agreed and she came to America. Ironically, in his letter Lane wrote that hearing people "must be endlessly vigilant against the disease of paternalism" (p. 153). This was written by a man who had decided to take a 10-year-old child away from her family and her native land because he had selected her to become the first deaf teacher in Burundi. Of the hundreds of thousands of adult deaf Africans, why did Lane pick a 10-year-old child to be the first teacher and tear her from her roots?

The complete story, as told by Lane, is a vivid display of arrogance. A man who has never been a classroom teacher of the deaf establishes "national" education of the deaf in a country where he does not know the national language, Kirundi. He receives no input from deaf professionals or organizations of the deaf. He selects as the first eventual deaf teacher of the deaf a 10-year-old child, who is shipped to the United States, where she will have no continued exposure to her national language. In various places. Lane refers to establishing "official" education, "national" education, and "formal" education for the deaf in Burundi. He uses the qualifying adjectives to diminish the fact that in reality a school for the deaf already existed upon his arrival in Burundi and that the teachers had been trained in Nigeria by a deaf African-American, Andrew Foster, the Laurent Clerc of education of the deaf in Africa.

The critical point is not whether Lane made the correct decision in sending the deaf child to the Model Secondary School for the Deaf [MSSD] in Washington, D.C., or sending the hearing trainee to Northeastern University. The point is that Lane made the decision arbitrarily and capriciously, without serious input from any professional, hearing or deaf. African or American. In fact, he ignored work that had already been done by Africans and by a deaf African-American. In the fifth paragraph of this review, I quoted Lane's opinion that there is an audist establishment that oppresses deaf people and that audism is the paternalistic hearing-centered endeavor that professes to serve deaf people but is really the hearing way of dominating, restructuring, and exercising authority over the deaf community. I don't believe there is an audist establishment, but there are audist individuals. By his behavior in Burundi, Lane reveals himself as a neo-colonialist and the quintessential audist.

In the final analysis, Lane speaks for neither the deaf community nor the hearing community -- like everyone else, he speaks only for himself. He chooses to believe that present-day problems in education of the deaf are due to efforts of an audist establishment that deliberately oppresses deaf people. The reviewer differs and believes that deaf and hearing educators of the deaf, like other human beings, tend to be complex individuals motivated by a number of factors, but that they are basically people of good will. Naivete, paternalism, and ignorance may abound, but deliberate repression is rare. Educators of the deaf really want to do right by the children entrusted to them.

As a person of intellect and good will, Lane will surely make significant contributions in the future. I hope the failure of *The Mask of Benevolence* is a temporary aberration in the work of a scholar.

References: **Allen, T., & Woodward, J. (1987)**. Teacher characteristics and the degree to which teachers incorporate features of English in their sign communication with hearing-impaired students. *American Annals of the Deaf 132*, 61-67. **Bowe, F. (1991)**. *Approaching equality: Education of the deaf*. Silver Spring, MD: T.J. Publishers. **Bowe, F. (1993)**. Approaching equality: A postscript. *American Annals of the Deaf* **Commission on Education of the Deaf. (1988)**. *Toward equality*: Education of the deaf. Washington, DC: U.S. Government Printing Office. **Gannon, J. R. (1981)**. *Deaf heritage: A narrative history of deaf America*. Silver Spring, MD: National Association of the Deaf **Moores, D (1992)**. *Least restrictive environment and education of deaf children: Testimony to the House of Representatives Subcommittee on Select Education. Washington, DC. Proceedings of the Third CAID* **(1853)**. Columbus, OH: Steam Press of Smith & Cox. **Proceedings of the 1858 CAID** Alton, IL: Courier Steam Book and Job Printing House. **Weed, G. L. (1859)**. The missionary element in deaf and dumb instruction, *Proceedings of the 1858 CAID*. Alton, IL: Courier Steam Book and Job Printing House.

[Reprinted with permission from Donald F. Moores. This review was also published in the American Annals of the Deaf]

Also available from Kodiak Media Group . . .

A CHILD SACRIFICED

TO THE DEAF CULTURE

INSTRUCTIONAL-CLASSROOM EDITION

By Tom Bertling

What others are saying about this book:

". . . A masterpiece . . . gripping . . . powerful . . . the author's outstanding legacy to the world."
>*-Prof. Frances Parsons,*
>**GALLAUDET UNIVERSITY**

". . . opened my eyes to a new perspective on cultural deafness...this information is vital to parents . . ."
>*--Thomas J. Balkany, MD, FACS*
>*Hotchkiss Distinguished Professor*
>**UNIVERSITY OF MIAMI**

"One hopes this book will be read by members of the deaf community with an eye towards critical self evaluation."
>*-Dr. Lloyd Lamb, Book Reviewer*
>**AMERICAN JOURNAL OF OTOLOGY**

"Tom Bertling swims where few dare to tread . . ."
>*-Paula Bonillas, Publisher and Editor*
>**HEARING HEALTH**

"A remarkable new book . . . at first hand, the author explains the motives of the deaf leaders . . . should be required reading . . ."
>*-Otto J. Menzel, Ph.D., Editor*
>**LIFE AFTER DEAFNESS**

NO DIGNITY FOR JOSHUA

By Tom Bertling

What others are saying about this book:

"Tom Bertling is the crusading knight who is challenging those fanatics, in defense of the coming generation of children who deserve a better fate than to be sacrificial pawns in a futile effort to preserve what those fanatics call "culture." If this be "genocide," make the most of it!"
-Otto J. Menzel, Ph.D., Editor
LIFE AFTER DEAFNESS

"Following the success of "A Child Sacrificed . . . ," Tom Bertling's second book "No Dignity for Joshua" continues the revelation by a "Deaf of Deaf" insider . . . His insights into the realities of the Deaf community, especially regarding sexual abuse of children, are disturbing. . . . Bertling's writing skills evidence the advantage of early exposure to hearing and even a short period of mainstreamed oral education. Tom Bertling is the conscience of the Deaf-World."
-Thomas J. Balkany, MD, FACS, FAAP
Hotchkiss Distinguished Professor
UNIVERSITY OF MIAMI

"From the oppression of deaf children to the bashing of Miss America, Bertling dissects the inner-workings of a small but powerful group who wield tremendous influence over our nation's culturally-deaf community. It is amazing to me how all this explosive material Bertling covers has missed the scrutiny of the mainstream press!"
-Paula Bonillas, Editor and Publisher
HEARING HEALTH

"The world needs more people like Tom Bertling to advocate on behalf of saving a crucial language for the deaf -- ENGLISH."
-Frances M. Parsons, Author
GALLAUDET UNIVERSITY

USE ORDER FORM ON THE NEXT PAGE

ASL: SHATTERING THE MYTH
NO DIGNITY FOR JOSHUA
A CHILD SACRIFICED

Order these books today!

QUAN.	BOOK TITLE	PRICE EACH	TOTAL
	"ASL: Shattering the Myth"	$19.95	
	"No Dignity for Joshua"	$21.95	
	"A Child Sacrificed"	$18.95	
		Handling fee	+ $4.95
		TOTAL DUE	

MAKE CHECK OR MONEY ORDER PAYABLE TO:
KODIAK MEDIA GROUP
PO BOX 1029-J3
WILSONVILLE, OREGON 97070

RUSH ORDERS MAILED WITHIN 5 BUSINESS DAYS, ADD $2.95 PER BOOK.
CANADIAN ORDERS, CHECK OR MONEY ORDER IN U.S. DOLLARS.
FOREIGN ORDERS, CHECK OR M/O IN US DOLLARS DRAWN ON A U.S. BANK.

PLEASE PRINT CLEARLY!

NAME_____

ADDRESS_____

CITY_____

STATE_____ZIP_____PH.(____)_____